Autodesk® Inventor® 2017
Design Variations and Representations

Student Guide
Mixed Units - 1st Edition

Authorized Publisher

ASCENT - Center for Technical Knowledge®
Autodesk® Inventor® 2017
Design Variations and Representations
Mixed Units - 1st Edition

Prepared and produced by:

ASCENT Center for Technical Knowledge
630 Peter Jefferson Parkway, Suite 175
Charlottesville, VA 22911

866-527-2368
www.ASCENTed.com

Lead Contributor: Jennifer MacMillan

ASCENT - Center for Technical Knowledge is a division of Rand Worldwide, Inc., providing custom developed knowledge products and services for leading engineering software applications. ASCENT is focused on specializing in the creation of education programs that incorporate the best of classroom learning and technology-based training offerings.

We welcome any comments you may have regarding this student guide, or any of our products. To contact us please email: feedback@ASCENTed.com.

Contents

Preface

The *Autodesk® Inventor® 2017: Design Variations and Representations* student guide contains topics that teach you how to efficiently create and represent designs based on existing geometry. Using this student guide, you will learn how the iFeature, iPart, and iAssembly tools can be used to leverage existing geometry to quickly and easily create additional or slightly varied geometry, and how iMates can be used to define geometry placement in an assembly.

The remaining chapters in the student guide focus on how you can simplify a model to create positional configurations to evaluate components' range of motion (Positional Representations), create simplified geometry to share with customers while protecting your intellectual property (Shrinkwrap and Assembly Simplification), and how to manage working with large assemblies (Level of Detail Representations).

The topics covered in this student guide are also covered in the following ASCENT student guides, which include a broader range of advanced topics:
- *Autodesk® Inventor® 2017: Advanced Assembly Modeling*
- *Autodesk® Inventor® 2017: Advanced Part Modeling*

Objectives

- Create and place an iFeature.
- Use the Copy command to duplicate features in a model or between models.
- Create a table-driven iFeature.
- Edit an iFeature.
- Create an iPart that can generate different configurations of a model.
- Insert standard or custom iParts into an assembly.
- Replace an iPart in an assembly with a new iPart instance.
- Modify an iPart factory.
- Use a table-driven iPart to create an iFeature.
- Build iMate constraints into parts or subassemblies.

- Combine multiple iMates into a Composite iMate group.
- Manually or automatically match iMates of parts in an assembly.
- Control the order in which iMate pairs are previewed by using the Match List functionality.
- Vary constraint settings in iParts by including iMates.
- Create and place an iAssembly.
- Edit an iAssembly Factory.
- Create and edit different positional representations of an assembly by overriding the existing settings of an assembly.
- Create a Shrinkwrap part that is a simplification of the original component.
- Selectively determine which assembly components to include in a simplified view and use that information to create a new part model.
- Define bounding box or cylindrical geometry to represent assembly components and use that information to create a new part model.
- Combine the use of a simplified view, envelopes, and visibility settings to create a new simplified model.
- Display a system-defined Level of Detail (LOD) Representation.
- Simplify the display and create user-defined LOD Representations in an assembly.
- Replace a complex component for a simpler one using a Substitute Level of Detail Representation.

Note on Software Setup

This student guide assumes a standard installation of the software using the default preferences during installation. Lectures and practices use the standard software templates and default options for the Content Libraries.

Students and Educators can Access Free Autodesk Software and Resources

Autodesk challenges you to get started with free educational licenses for professional software and creativity apps used by millions of architects, engineers, designers, and hobbyists today. Bring Autodesk software into your classroom, studio, or workshop to learn, teach, and explore real-world design challenges the way professionals do.

Get started today - register at the Autodesk Education Community and download one of the many Autodesk software applications available.

Visit www.autodesk.com/joinedu/

Note: Free products are subject to the terms and conditions of the end-user license and services agreement that accompanies the software. The software is for personal use for education purposes and is not intended for classroom or lab use.

Lead Contributor: Jennifer MacMillan

With a dedication for engineering and education, Jennifer has spent over 20 years at ASCENT managing courseware development for various CAD products. Trained in Instructional Design, Jennifer uses her skills to develop instructor-led and web-based training products as well as knowledge profiling tools.

Jennifer has achieved the Autodesk Certified Professional certification for Inventor and is also recognized as an Autodesk Certified Instructor (ACI). She enjoys teaching the training courses that she authors and is also very skilled in providing technical support to end-users.

Jennifer holds a Bachelor of Engineering Degree as well as a Bachelor of Science in Mathematics from Dalhousie University, Nova Scotia, Canada.

Jennifer MacMillan has been the Lead Contributor for *Autodesk Inventor: Design Variations and Representations* since its initial release in 2017.

In this Guide

The following images highlight some of the features that can be found in this Student Guide.

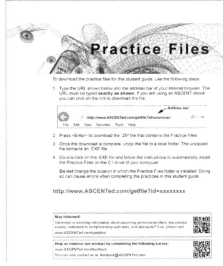

FTP link for practice files

Practice Files

The Practice Files page tells you how to download and install the practice files that are provided with this student guide.

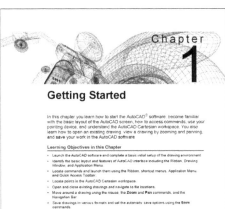

Learning Objectives for the chapter

Chapters

Each chapter begins with a brief introduction and a list of the chapter's Learning Objectives.

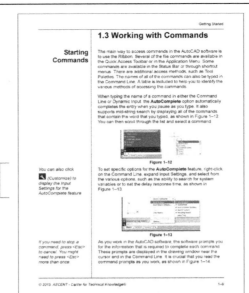

Instructional Content

Each chapter is split into a series of sections of instructional content on specific topics. These lectures include the descriptions, step-by-step procedures, figures, hints, and information you need to achieve the chapter's Learning Objectives.

Side notes

Side notes are hints or additional information for the current topic.

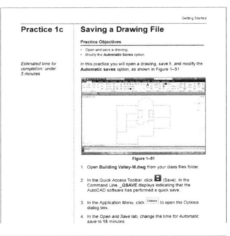

Practice Objectives

Practices

Practices enable you to use the software to perform a hands-on review of a topic.

Some practices require you to use prepared practice files, which can be downloaded from the link found on the Practice Files page.

Chapter Review Questions

Chapter review questions, located at the end of each chapter, enable you to review the key concepts and learning objectives of the chapter.

Command Summary

The Command Summary is located at the end of each chapter. It contains a list of the software commands that are used throughout the chapter, and provides information on where the command is found in the software.

Icons in this Student Guide

The following icons are used to help you quickly and easily find helpful information.

Indicates items that are new in the Autodesk Inventor 2017 software.

Indicates items that have been enhanced in the Autodesk Inventor 2017 software.

Practice Files

To download the practice files for this student guide, use the following steps:

1. Type the URL shown below into the address bar of your Internet browser. The URL must be typed **exactly as shown**. If you are using an ASCENT ebook, you can click on the link to download the file.

Address bar

http://www.ascented.com/getfile?id=anguis

File   Edit   View   Favorites   Tools   Help

2. Press <Enter> to download the .ZIP file that contains the Practice Files.

3. Once the download is complete, unzip the file to a local folder. The unzipped file contains an .EXE file.

4. Double-click on the .EXE file and follow the instructions to automatically install the Practice Files on the C:\ drive of your computer.

   Do not change the location in which the Practice Files folder is installed. Doing so can cause errors when completing the practices in this student guide.

http://www.ascented.com/getfile?id=anguis

Stay Informed!

Interested in receiving information about upcoming promotional offers, educational events, invitations to complimentary webcasts, and discounts? If so, please visit:

www.ASCENTed.com/updates/

Help us improve our product by completing the following survey:

www.ASCENTed.com/feedback

You can also contact us at: *feedback@ASCENTed.com*

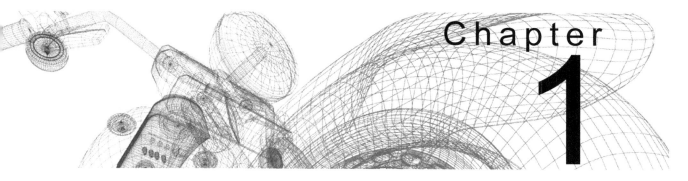

Copying Between Parts (iFeatures)

The Autodesk® Inventor® software provides several methods to copy features between models. One of these methods involves the use of iFeatures. This duplication technique helps to reduce the amount of time spent duplicating a collection of features or components that are used repeatedly in an individual model, or across several models.

Learning Objectives in this Chapter

- Create an iFeature by selecting the features, parameters, and placement elements to define the iFeature.
- Place an iFeature by defining its placement plane, size values, and precise positioning to fully locate it in a model.
- Use the Copy command to duplicate features in a model or between models.
- Create a table-driven iFeature that includes variations that can be retrieved during the placement of the iFeature.
- Edit the size, position, and sketch location of an iFeature that has been placed in a model.
- Edit a source iFeature file to make changes to its initial definition.

1.1 Creating iFeatures

When you create parts, you may require the same type of feature in multiple parts. By using iFeatures as part of your design process you can save any sketched feature for use in other part files. Using iFeatures saves time and helps ensure consistency between parts. iFeatures are stored in files with the extension .IDE. By default, they are stored in the *C:\Users\Public\ Public Documents\Autodesk\ Inventor 2017\Catalog* directory. Several predefined iFeatures are installed with the Autodesk Inventor software and are stored in this directory.

General Steps

Use the following general steps to create an iFeature:

1. Start the creation of an iFeature.
2. Select features to save as iFeatures.
3. Set the parameter size.
4. Define the iFeature position geometry.
5. Save the iFeature.

Step 1 - Start the creation of an iFeature.

Open the part that contains the sketches and features you want to use. In the *Manage* tab>Author panel, click 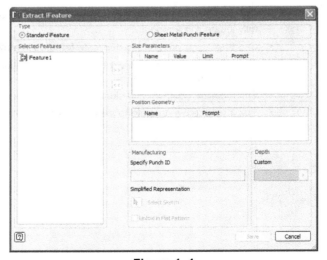 (Extract iFeature). The Extract iFeature dialog box opens, as shown in Figure 1–1.

Figure 1–1

Step 2 - Select features to save as iFeatures.

Select sketches and features in the Model browser or graphics window that are to become iFeatures. You can select unconsumed or consumed sketches. If the selected feature has dependent features, they are automatically selected. All elements used to create the selected feature appear below the name of the iFeature in the Selected Features area, as shown in Figure 1–2. You can use any or all of the part features in the iFeature.

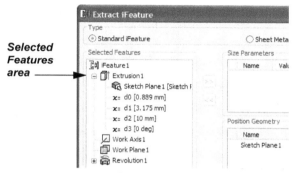

Selected Features area

Figure 1–2

*To rename an iFeature so that its name in the Model browser is descriptive, right-click on the iFeature# at the top of the Selected Features column and select **Rename**. Enter a new name. This name identifies the iFeature whenever it is placed. Renaming the iFeature is different from naming the iFeature's .IDE filename.*

The dialog box auto populates the *Size Parameters* and *Position Geometry* areas with any renamed parameters. To add other feature parameters that are to be used in the iFeature, select them in the *Selected Features* area and use the ⟩⟩ icon to transfer the parameters one by one. To add all parameters associated with a feature, select the feature and select **Add All Parameters** in the shortcut menu. Figure 1–3 shows all Extrusion1 parameters transferred to the *Size Parameters* area.

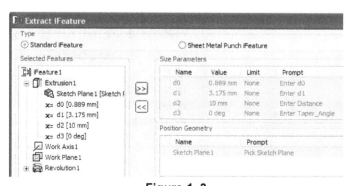

Figure 1–3

To remove a feature from a list, select the feature and select **Remove Feature** in the shortcut menu. To remove parameters, use the ⌐≪ icon to return the parameters to the *Selected Features* area, or select **Remove All Parameters** in the shortcut menu.

Step 3 - Set the parameter size.

Once the feature parameters are transferred to the *Size Parameters* area of the dialog box you can control the size of the iFeature by applying a range or limits to the parameters. The *Size Parameters* area consists of four columns, described as follows:

Name	Lists the name of the parameter that describes a dimension of the feature. You can change the name of the parameter by selecting on it. Use a name that is descriptive to help when reusing the iFeature.
Value	Displays the default value for the parameter.
Limit	Enables you to restrict the values of parameters using the following three options:
None	Any value is acceptable.
Range	Set the allowable range for the value by entering the upper and lower values and the operator.
List	Enables you to create a group of acceptable values and set the default value of the parameter.
Prompt	Enables you to set the text that displays in a dialog box when the iFeature is inserted. You can enter information that clarifies the use of the value or describes restrictions.

Step 4 - Define the iFeature position geometry.

In the Extract iFeature dialog box, the *Position Geometry* area specifies the elements in the iFeature that are used to locate it on a part. The Sketch Plane is automatically added to this area. You can add or remove other items, such as constraints from the feature, using the ⌐≫ and ⌐≪ icons.

An iFeature should contain geometry that is only dependent on the geometry in the iFeature itself. Do not use Origin work features. Horizontal and vertical constraints can make it difficult to place an iFeature, because those terms are relative to the part where the feature is placed. Use parallel and perpendicular constraints instead.

The *Position Geometry* area consists of two columns, described as follows:

Name	Names the position geometry. You can change it here, but it does not change the name in the Selected Features area.
Prompt	Defines the text prompt that is provided when the iFeature is inserted. You can enter information that prompts you where to select on the existing part to place the iFeature.

You might need to customize position geometry (for example, combine two location geometries, or make one position independent of the other). Right-click on the position in the *Position Geometry* area and select **Combine Geometry**, then select another position to combine. To make positions in a combined geometry independent, right-click on the combined position and select **Make Independent**.

Step 5 - Save the iFeature.

By default, iFeatures are saved in the *Catalog* folder (*C:\Users\Public\ Public Documents\Autodesk\Inventor 2017\ Catalog*) or you can create a new folder in this *Catalog* folder to further organize the files. Once the iFeature is defined and its locating position determined, in the Extract iFeature dialog box, click **Save**. The Save As dialog box opens. Enter a unique name for the iFeature and click **Save** and close the dialog box. All iFeatures are saved with the extension .IDE.

1.2 Inserting iFeatures

An iFeature can be placed in the same part in which it was created or it can be placed in any other part, as shown in Figure 1–4.

An iFeature reduces the time spent on duplicating a collection of features or components that are used repeatedly in the same or in different models.

iFeature is duplicated in a model

iFeature is inserted in a different model

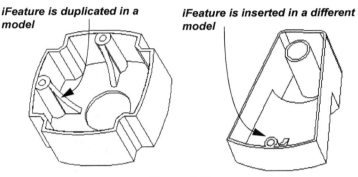

Figure 1–4

General Steps

Use the following general steps to place an iFeature:

1. Start the placement of the iFeature.
2. Select the position of the iFeature.
3. Determine the size of the iFeature.
4. Determine the precise position.
5. Complete the insertion.

Step 1 - Start the placement of the iFeature.

You can also drag an iFeature from Windows Explorer to the main window.

In the *Manage* tab>Insert panel, click 🔲 (Insert iFeature). Click **Browse** and browse to the iFeature, select, and open the iFeature. By default, iFeatures are saved in the *Catalog* folder (*C:\Users\Public\Public Documents\Autodesk\Inventor 2017\Catalog*).

As an alternative to initiating the **Insert iFeature** option and selecting an iFeature, you can select an iFeature directly from the ribbon. All iFeatures stored in the Catalog are listed in the drop-down list, as shown in Figure 1–5. Scroll through the list and select the iFeature.

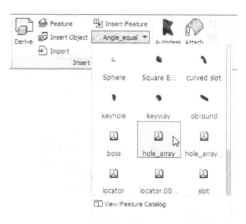

Figure 1–5

Step 2 - Select the position of the iFeature.

*Once the iFeature is open, a green symbol on the left side of the Insert **iFeature** dialog box shows you that you are in the "Position" step.*

The Position step enables you to select a planar face or work plane to locate the feature. Once you select the plane, you can select the rotation or the position symbol, shown in Figure 1–6, to rotate or move the iFeature, as required.

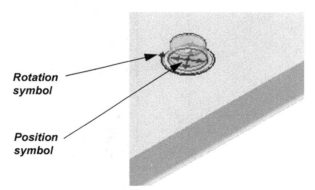

Rotation symbol

Position symbol

Figure 1–6

Alternatively, you can enter a rotation angle in the dialog box.

Click ✎ to flip the direction of the iFeature. A checkmark displays to the left of the name of the feature or sketch when the placement for the iFeature is fully defined, as shown in Figure 1–7.

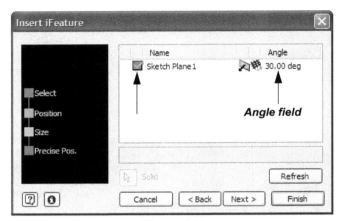

Figure 1–7

Step 3 - Determine the size of the iFeature.

Once the position is defined, click **Next** to move to the Size step. The Size step lists the names and default values of the parameters of the iFeatures. An example is shown in Figure 1–8.

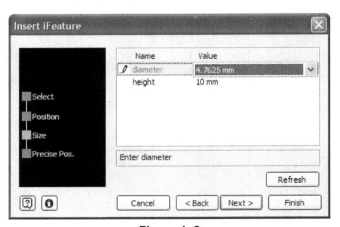

Figure 1–8

Select a value to change it. Once you change the size, click **Refresh** in the dialog box to update the display of the iFeature.

Step 4 - Determine the precise position.

Once the sizes are defined, click **Next** to move to the Precise Pos. step. The Insert iFeature dialog box displays as shown in Figure 1–9.

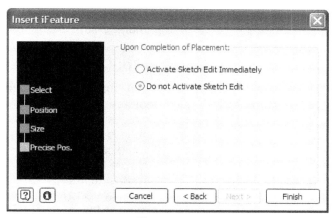

Figure 1–9

The Precise Pos. step determines what happens when the operation is complete.

- If you select **Activate Sketch Edit Immediately**, **Edit Sketch** is activated so that you can locate the sketch precisely before you continue with the part.

- If you select **Do not Activate Sketch Edit**, **iFeature** is added without accessing the sketch environment.

You can move back and forth through the steps using **Next** and **Back**, or by selecting the steps in the tree graphic.

Once the location and size of the iFeature are defined, click **Finish** to complete the operation. Depending on the option that was selected in the Precise Pos. step, the sketch environment might open to refine the iFeature's placement.

- No link exists between the .IDE file and the iFeature once the iFeature is placed. Therefore, changes to the .IDE file do not affect iFeatures that are already placed. Even if you insert a revised iFeature into a file that contains an older version of the feature, the original iFeature is not affected. To update a placed iFeature, delete the old iFeature and insert the new one.

1.3 iFeatures vs. Copy Feature

Some features in your models can be simply copied and pasted as a means of duplicating them within or to another model. For those features that cannot be copied, you can use iFeatures. In general, features that have sketched sections can be copied; however, features that are located on surface or reference edges (e.g., holes, fillets, shells) cannot be copied.

How To: Copy and Paste a Feature

1. Verify that the **Select Features** filter is enabled and select the feature in the model or the Model browser.
2. Once selected, right-click and select **Copy**. If the **Copy** option is not available, this action is not permitted and you should consider recreating the feature or using an iFeature.
3. Activate the model that is to be the target model, if it is not already the active model.
4. Right-click and select **Paste**. A Paste Features dialog box similar to that shown in Figure 1–10 opens, indicating the references required to place the feature.

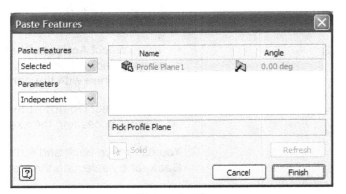

Figure 1–10

5. Select a *Parameters* option. This enables you to define whether the copied feature is dependent or independent. If the feature is copied in the same model, you can select whether or not the new feature is dependent on the source feature. If you are copying to a new model, the copied feature can only be independent.
6. Define the placement reference for the copied feature.
7. Click **Finish**. Depending on the placement references that were defined, you might need to further edit the feature to fully locate it in the model.

1.4 Table-Driven iFeatures

iFeatures are made up of parameters independent of each other, unless they are related by an equation. Table-driven iFeatures provide additional control by presetting these parameters to permitted values. For example, a threaded stud can be an iFeature. The diameter of the stud may have several preset values, and each diameter, preset lengths. Not all lengths apply to all of the diameters; therefore, you can change the iFeature to allow only certain lengths. Through the use of keys in a Table-driven iFeature you can logically group the iFeature members to enable quicker access to the required configuration.

General Steps

Use the following general steps to create a table-driven iFeature:

1. Open the iFeature file.
2. Select the configurable attributes.
3. Create the table.
4. Set up keys.
5. Complete the table.

Step 1 - Open the iFeature file.

Open an iFeature. In the iFeature panel, click 📝 (iFeature Author Table). The dialog box opens as shown in Figure 1–11.

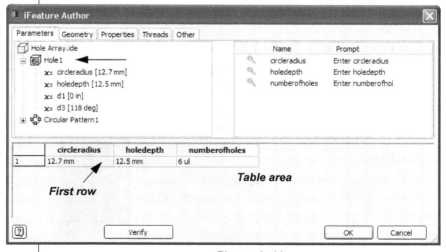

Figure 1–11

Step 2 - Select the configurable attributes.

The tabs in the iFeature Author dialog box contain the configurable attributes that can be varied to create the different iFeature configurations.

*To create a custom property in an iFeature, open the iFeature, right-click on the iFeature name in the Model browser, and select **iProperties**. Select the Custom tab and create any custom properties that are required.*

Tabs	Description
Parameters tab	Contains the parameters used in the part and they are listed under the features in which they belong. Parameters that have names other than d# are listed automatically in the Selected Parameters list.
Geometry tab	Displays the geometry used to position the iFeature. You can change the names and prompts for the geometry in this tab.
Properties tab	Lists the properties of the feature. Any custom properties in an iFeature can be made available in the Part files in which they are inserted. In the *Properties* tab, expand the **Custom** node and select the required custom parameter, then add it to the table as a property using the arrow icons. Once a property has been moved to the right side of the dialog box, you can set keys on these properties.
Threads tab	Enables you to include thread variables. Each thread variable is defined as a key. Designations such as UNC are case-sensitive.
Other tab	Enables you to create additional columns in the table. These columns do not control the size of the part, but can be used as keys in the table.

You can insert the iFeature with any of the attribute values that were set in the iFeature Author dialog box. For example, you can insert an iFeature with the hole depth parameter values shown in Figure 1–12.

Table area of iFeature Author dialog box

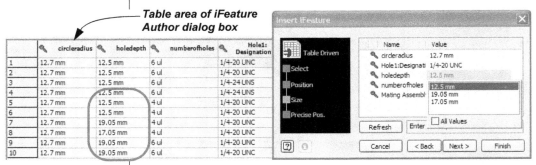

	circleradius	holedepth	numberofholes	Hole1: Designation
1	12.7 mm	12.5 mm	6 ul	1/4-20 UNC
2	12.7 mm	12.5 mm	6 ul	1/4-20 UNC
3	12.7 mm	12.5 mm	6 ul	1/4-24 UNS
4	12.7 mm	12.5 mm	6 ul	1/4-24 UNS
5	12.7 mm	12.5 mm	4 ul	1/4-20 UNC
6	12.7 mm	12.5 mm	4 ul	1/4-20 UNC
7	12.7 mm	19.05 mm	4 ul	1/4-20 UNC
8	12.7 mm	17.05 mm	4 ul	1/4-20 UNC
9	12.7 mm	19.05 mm	6 ul	1/4-20 UNC
10	12.7 mm	19.05 mm	6 ul	1/4-20 UNC

Figure 1–12

You can also enter custom values (ones not predefined) for an attribute by setting its column as custom. This enables you to enter custom values when the iFeature is inserted.

How To: Enter Custom Attribute Values

1. Right-click the attribute column in the table and select **Key> Not A Key** if a key is assigned to the parameter.
2. Right-click the attribute column in the table and select **Custom Parameter Column**. The column displays in blue.

The shortcut menu is shown in Figure 1–13.

You can also control permitted values for an attribute by defining a range and/or increment.

You customize the cell, before applying a range or increment to it

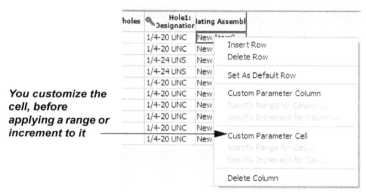

Figure 1–13

Step 3 - Create the table.

It is possible to edit the iFeature table in a spread sheet format using (Edit Using Spread Sheet).

Each row in the table represents a different version of the iFeature. To add more versions, right-click in the first row and select **Insert Row**. Select the table cells and enter the attribute values for each cell. Once filled in, the table area displays similar to that shown in Figure 1–14.

	circleradius	holedepth	numberofholes	Hole1: Designation	Mating Assembly
1	12.7 mm	12.5 mm	6 ul	1/4-20 UNC	New Item0
2	12.7 mm	12.5 mm	6 ul	1/4-20 UNC	New Item0
3	12.7 mm	12.5 mm	6 ul	1/4-24 UNS	New Item0
4	12.7 mm	12.5 mm	6 ul	1/4-24 UNS	New Item0
5	12.7 mm	12.5 mm	4 ul	1/4-20 UNC	New Item0
6	12.7 mm	12.5 mm	4 ul	1/4-20 UNC	New Item0
7	12.7 mm	19.05 mm	4 ul	1/4-20 UNC	New Item0
8	12.7 mm	17.05 mm	4 ul	1/4-20 UNC	New Item0
9	12.7 mm	19.05 mm	6 ul	1/4-20 UNC	New Item0
10	12.7 mm	19.05 mm	6 ul	1/4-20 UNC	New Item0

Figure 1–14

Step 4 - Set up keys.

An iFeature contains attribute values that define each iFeature member. Keys enable you to group iFeature members according to their attribute values in a hierarchical manner. This sorts the iFeature members more logically, enabling quicker access to the required configuration. A key ✎ symbol displays in front of each attribute in the iFeature Author dialog box. Toggle the key symbols on (blue) and off (gray) to define a particular attribute as a key. For the attributes you set as keys, assign the key order (starting from 1 as the first key). The attribute set as Key 1 is the first attribute that is used for sorting or grouping the iFeature members. If Length was the first key, then all the iFeature members will be sorted according to length. To change the order of key numbers, or to assign a key number to an attribute, right-click it and select **Key** and the required number, as shown in Figure 1–15.

You can customize the name displayed in the Model browser for an iFeature to show the Key1 parameter name and its value. Select **Use Key 1 as Browser Name column** *in the Application Options dialog box (iFeature tab). This helps identify which iFeature value set is used.*

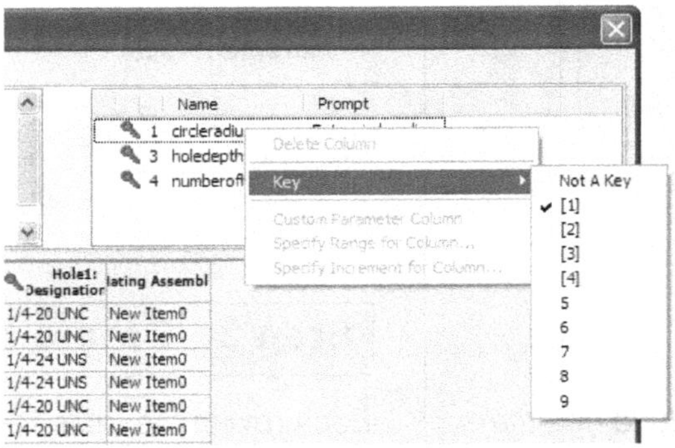

Figure 1–15

If five members had the same length of 500mm, then all five would be listed under that length (length = 500mm) in the Model browser. Next, the members are sorted according to the second key, for example width. The five members with length=500mm would be grouped according to width. If two of those members had widths of 100mm and the other three had widths of 150mm, then they would be sorted under width = 100mm and width = 150mm. The sorting continues until no more keys are defined.

Step 5 - Complete the table.

Once the table is defined, click **OK** to complete the operation.

1.5 Editing iFeatures

Edit Inserted iFeature

Once the iFeature is inserted, you can only edit its size, position, and sketch location on the sketch plane. To edit the size and position, right-click on the iFeature and select **Edit iFeature**. To edit the sketch location, right-click on the iFeature and select **Edit Sketch**. You can add dimensions and constraints; however, not change its dimensions.

Edit iFeature file

You might need to change the iFeature file (.IDE) once it has been created. To do so, open the iFeature file in a separate window. The iFeature panel displays as shown in Figure 1–16.

The ⌐ (Edit iFeature) option enables you to modify sizes and position.

Figure 1–16

To view stored iFeatures, including standard predefined

iFeatures, in the iFeature panel, click ⌐ (View Catalog). The Catalog viewer displays in a standard Windows Explorer view, as shown in Figure 1–17.

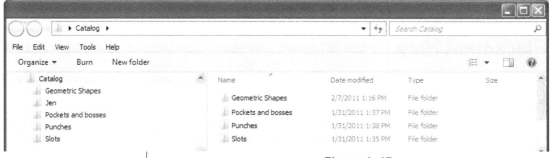

Figure 1–17

Tables are covered in more detail in table-driven iFeatures.

Click ⌐ (iFeature Author Table) to create or modify iFeature

tables. If an iFeature table is used, you can use ⌐ (Edit Using Spread Sheet) to edit the values in a spread sheet format.

Editing the iFeature Image

When an iFeature is created, it is assigned the default icon image (⌸). This image identifies the iFeature in the Model browser of any part that you place it in, as well as in the ribbon when selecting the iFeature from the Insert panel. You may want to change the iFeature image to help identify it in the Model browser. To do this, open the iFeature file in a separate window and in the iFeature panel, click (Change Icon). The Edit Icon dialog box opens as shown in Figure 1–18.

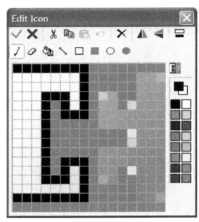

Figure 1–18

Using the colors and the tools in the dialog box, create a new image to represent the iFeature. To obtain a white background, you must use the Magenta color in all areas that are required to be displayed as white. Once the icon is complete, save the .IDE file. The new icon will display once you restart the Autodesk Inventor software.

Placement Help

You can create a separate document to help describe, to future users of the iFeature, how it is to be placed and used in a model. To attach a placement help file, open the iFeature's .IDE file and on the *Tools* tab>Insert panel, click (Insert Object). Select **Create from File** and click **Browse** to browse to the document. Click **Open** when you have selected the required document.

The placement help file can be added as a linked or an embedded object. Embedded objects are not dependent on the external file, whereas linked files are dependent. Click **OK**. The file displays in the Model browser, as shown in Figure 1–19.

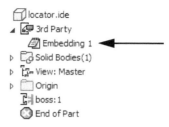

Figure 1–19

In the Model browser, right-click on the placement help file and select **Placement Help** to set this as the placement help document. Save the iFeature file.

To open the placement help file, double-click on the file in the Model browser.

Practice 1a	# Create and Insert an iFeature

Practice Objectives

- Assign parameter names and equations to existing dimensions in a model to prepare for iFeature creation.
- Create an iFeature from existing geometry so that a limit and range is established for selected iFeature dimensional values and an appropriate prompt is defined for the placement plane.
- Insert a placement help file to be used as a reference for locating an iFeature in a model.
- Insert an iFeature into a new part file.

In this practice, you create an iFeature. You set the limits for the iFeature's sketch diameter and set a range for one of the features' height. You then place help text in the iFeature file to help insert it. The completed model is shown in Figure 1–20.

Figure 1–20

Task 1 - Change the name of model parameters.

iFeatures are created from existing features or sketches. To make it easier to create the iFeature, use parameters that have descriptive names and apply those parameters to items in the sketches and features that will become your iFeature. Creating an iFeature with default parameters (such as d0) can be confusing to identify. In this task, you change the name of model parameters (dimensions).

This project file is used for the entire training guide.

1. In the *Get Started* tab>Launch panel, click 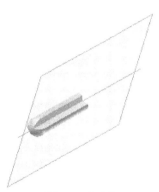 (Projects) to open the Projects dialog box. Project files identify folders that contain the required models.

2. Click **Browse**. In the *C:\Autodesk Inventor 2017 Design Variations and Representations Exercise Files* folder, select **Design Variations and Representations.ipj**. Click **Open**. The Projects dialog box updates and a check mark displays next to the new project name, indicating that it is the active project. The project file tells Autodesk Inventor where your files are stored. Click **Done**.

3. In the Quick Access Toolbar, click .

4. Select **createif.ipt** and click **Open**. The model displays as shown in Figure 1–21.

Figure 1–21

5. In the *Manage* tab>Parameter panel, click f_x (Parameters) to open the Parameters dialog box.

6. Change the names of parameters as follows:
    *   *d1* to **diameter**
    *   *d2* to **height**

Plan your iFeatures so that a minimum number of parameters are required. If a dimension is always half of another dimension, use an equation rather than forcing you to enter both numbers.

7. Change the equations as follows:
   - *d0* to **diameter/3**
   - *d4* to **diameter/2**

The Parameters dialog box displays as shown in Figure 1–22.

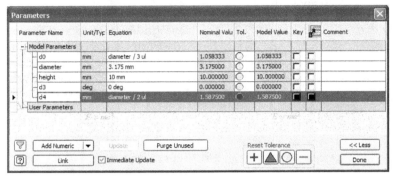

Figure 1–22

8. Click **Done** to close the dialog box.

Task 2 - Create an iFeature.

---

1. In the *Manage* tab>Author panel, click 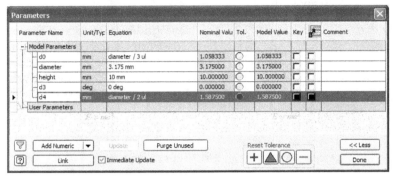 (Extract iFeature) to open the Extract iFeature dialog box.

2. Select **Extrusion1** in the Model browser. The *Selected Features* area displays **Extrusion1**, **Revolution1**, and the work features because the other features are children. The renamed parameters are automatically entered in the *Size Parameters* area and the **Extrusion1** sketch plane is displayed in the *Position Geometry* area. The Extract iFeature dialog box displays as shown in Figure 1–23.

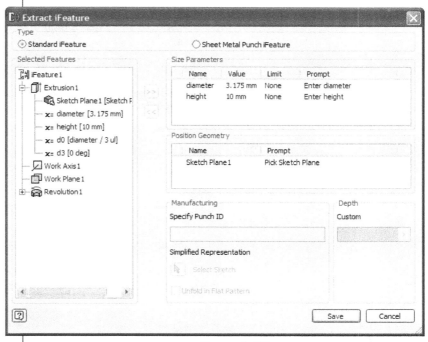

Figure 1–23

3. Note that the Limit for both parameters is set to **None**. Select **None** for the diameter parameter, and select **List** in the drop-down list. The List Values for the diameter dialog box opens.

4. Select **Click here to add value** at the bottom of the list and add the following diameters: **1.5875**, **4.7625**, **6.35**, **9.525**.

5. Set **4.7625** as the *Default*, as shown in Figure 1–24.

Figure 1–24

6. Click **OK** to close the dialog box.

7. Select **None** for the height parameter, and select **Range** in the drop-down list. The Specify Range for the height dialog box opens.

8. Set the *Range* to **2.5<10<25**, as shown in Figure 1–25.

Figure 1–25

9. Click **OK** to close the dialog box.

10. Change the *Prompt* for **Sketch Plane1** to **Pick plane for base of locator**, as shown in Figure 1–26.

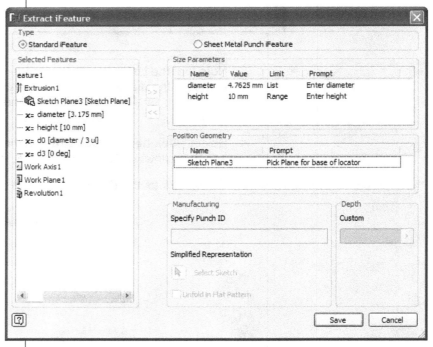

Figure 1–26

11. Right-click on **iFeature1** at the top of the *Selected Features* pane and select **Rename**. Enter **boss** as the new name. This name will be used to identify the iFeature in a Model browser whenever it is placed.

Renaming the iFeature is different from naming the iFeature's .IDE filename.

Once the iFeature is defined and its locating position is determined, it is saved in the *Catalog* folder. Alternatively, you can create a new folder in the *Catalog* folder to save your iFeatures.

12. In the Extract iFeature dialog box, click **Save**. The Save As dialog box opens.

13. In the Save As dialog, ensure that you are in the *Catalog* folder. Right-click in the white area, and select **New>Folder**. Create a new folder in the *Catalog* folder with your own name. Store your iFeatures in this folder.

14. Double-click on the new folder, type the name **locator** for the iFeature filename, and click **Save** to save the iFeature. iFeatures are saved with the extension .IDE.

15. Close the createif.ipt file. You do not need to save the changes, since they are already saved in the catalog.

Task 3 - Insert a placement help file in iFeature.

1. Open the file **locator.ide** that you just created (*C:\Users\Public\Public Documents\Autodesk\Inventor 2017\Catalog\<yourname>* folder or the specified path that was used on your computer).

2. In the *Tools* tab>Insert panel, click 🔲↵ (Insert Object) to open the Insert Object dialog box.

3. Select **Create from File** and click **Browse** to browse to the **locator.doc** file in your practice files folder. Click **Open**. This file is a Placement Help file that can be added as a linked or an embedded object. Embedded objects are not dependent on the external file, whereas linked files are dependent.

4. Click **OK**. Expand the 3**rd Party** node and the file displays in the Model browser, as shown in Figure 1–27.

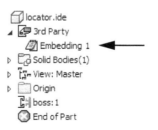

Figure 1–27

5. Right-click on **Embedding 1** in the Model browser, and select **Placement Help** to set this as the placement help document.

6. Save the iFeature file and close the window. You cannot insert an open iFeature.

Task 4 - Insert an iFeature.

In this task, you insert and place the locator.ide file into a part.

1. Open **fanbase.ipt**.

2. In the *Manage* tab>Insert panel, click ⬛ (Insert iFeature).

3. Browse to and open the **locator.ide** file.

   The green symbol in the graphic on the left side of the Insert iFeature dialog box indicates that you are in the Position step. This step enables you to select a face to locate the feature. Once you select the face, you can select the rotation or the position symbol to rotate or move the part. Alternatively, you can type the rotation angle in the fields.

4. Select the face shown in Figure 1–28 as the position plane.

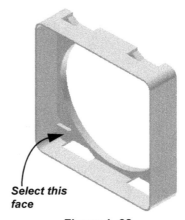

Select this face

Figure 1–28

   A checkmark displays to the left of the name of the feature or sketch when the placement for the iFeature has been fully defined.

5. Once the position is defined, click **Next** to move to the Size step. The Size step lists the names and default values of the parameters for locator.ide, as shown in Figure 1–29.

Figure 1–29

6. Note that the diameter *Value* column shows the default, **4.7625mm**.

7. Enter **8mm** in the height *Value* column. Remember the height range is between 2.5mm and 25mm.

8. Once you select the size, click **Refresh** to update the iFeature on the screen.

9. Click **Next** to move to Precise Pos. step.

10. Click 🔘 to open **locator.doc**, as shown in Figure 1–30.

The Precise Pos. step determines what happens when the command is completed.

Instructions for Placement of the LOCATOR:

[Move the iFeature sketch to the center of the arc shown below and constrain the center of the sketch to the center of arc shown below. This will fully locate the iFeature]

end

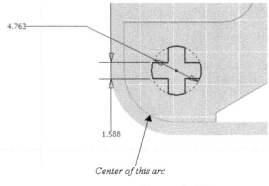

Figure 1–30

11. Read the instructions on how to locate the locator.ide.

12. Close **locator.doc**.

13. Select **Activate Sketch Edit Immediately** to activate **Edit Sketch**.

---

14. Click **Finish** to complete the operation.

There is no link between the .IDE file and the iFeature once the iFeature is placed. Therefore, changes to the .IDE file do not affect iFeatures that are already placed. Even if you insert a revised iFeature into a file that contains an older version of the feature, the original iFeature is not affected. To update an already placed iFeature, delete the old iFeature and insert the new one.

15. Locate the iFeature sketch according to the instructions and exit the sketch. The locator displays on the model, as shown in Figure 1–31. The placement help file displays in the **fanbase.ipt** part Model browser, where you can edit it.

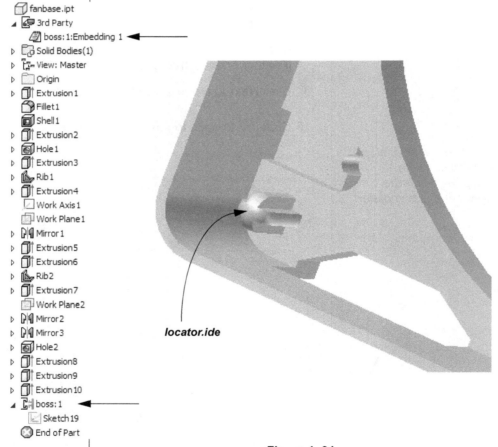

locator.ide

Figure 1–31

Note that although you inserted the **locator.ide** iFeature, the iFeature is identified in the Model browser as boss.

16. Insert three instances of **locator.ide** in the three corners of **fanbase.ipt**. Select the same plane as before for the position. Try to set the height of the feature to **30mm**. Since it is outside the specified range, the value is not allowed. Change the diameter; note that you can select from the values you specified in the list.

17. Save and close the model.

Practice 1b

Table-Driven iFeature

Practice Objectives

- Create an iFeature that is driven by a table defining the possible variations that can be retrieved during placement.
- Insert a table driven iFeature into a new part file.
- Edit a placed iFeature to change the table instance that was inserted into a new part file.

In this practice, you create a table-driven iFeature from a hole pattern, and use the iFeature in a part. The final model displays as shown in Figure 1–32.

Figure 1–32

Task 1 - Create an iFeature.

1. Open **circle.ipt**.

2. In the *Manage* tab>Author panel, click  (Extract iFeature) to open the Extract iFeature dialog box.

3. In the Model browser, select **Hole1** (**Circular Pattern2** is automatically selected with **Hole1** because it is a child of Hole1). The Extract iFeature dialog box displays as shown in Figure 1–33.

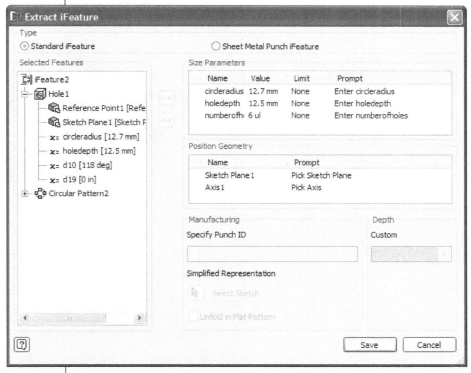

Figure 1–33

4. At the top of the *Selected Features* pane, right-click on **iFeature2** and select **Rename**. Enter **hole_array** as the new name.

5. In the Extract iFeature dialog box, click **Save**.

6. Save the file as **hole_array** in the *C:\....\Catalog\<yourname>* folder.

7. Close **circle.ipt**. You do not need to save the changes, since they are already saved in the catalog.

Task 2 - Create a table-driven iFeature.

1. Open **hole_array.ide** (*C:\Users\Public\ Public Documents\ Autodesk\Inventor 2017\Catalog \<yourname>* folder or the specified path that was used on your computer). The iFeature file only contains the selected features, as shown in Figure 1–34.

Figure 1–34

2. In the *iFeature* tab>iFeature panel, click 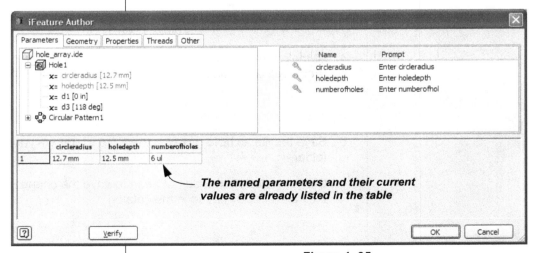 (iFeature Author Table). The dialog box opens as shown in Figure 1–35. The named parameters and their values are already listed.

Figure 1–35

3. Select the *Threads* tab and copy **Hole1: Designation** from the left to the right side using the >> icon to add it as a column in the table.

4. Select the *Other* tab. Click **Click here to add a value** if a value doesn't already exist in the right-hand column. Enter **Mating Assembly** as the *Name* and **Mating Assembly** for the *Prompt*, as shown in Figure 1–36. It is added as a column.

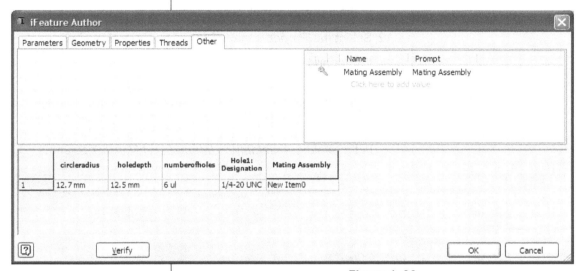

Figure 1–36

5. Select the *circleradius* column header, right-click, and select **Key>1** in the shortcut menu. Then, do the following:

   • Assign Key 2 to the *Hole1:Designation* column.
   • Assign Key 3 to the *holedepth* column.
   • Assign Key 4 to the *numberofholes* column.

6. Verify that the *Mating Assembly* column is not defined as a key by right-clicking the column header and selecting **Key>Not a Key**.

7. To enter custom values in the *Mating Assembly* column you must set it as a custom parameter. Right-click on the *Mating Assembly* column header and select **Custom Parameter Column**.

8. Select the *Properties* tab. Currently, no custom properties are listed. You must first assign a custom property to the .IDE file. Click **OK** to close the iFeature Author dialog box.

9. In the Model browser, right-click on **hole_array.ide** and select **iProperties**. Select the *Custom* tab.

10. Enter **Internal Drill Number** as the name, accept **Text** as the type, and enter **IDN7** as the value. Click **Add** and click **OK**.

11. In the iFeature panel, click ⬚ (iFeature Author Table).

12. Select the *Properties* tab. Expand Custom at the bottom of the list and use ⬚ to add *Internal Drill Number* as a property.

13. Select the first row and select **Insert Row** in the shortcut menu. Add 8 additional rows for a total of 10 rows. Edit the table values as shown in Figure 1–37. No edits are required in the *Mating Assembly* or *Internal Drill Number* columns.

	circleradius	holedepth	numberofholes	Hole1: Designation	Mating Assembly	Internal Drill Number
1	12.7 mm	12.5 mm	6 ul	1/4-20 UNC	New Item0	IDN7
2	12.7 mm	12.5 mm	6 ul	1/4-20 UNC	New Item0	IDN7
3	12.7 mm	12.5 mm	6 ul	1/4-24 UNS	New Item0	IDN7
4	12.7 mm	12.5 mm	6 ul	1/4-24 UNS	New Item0	IDN7
5	12.7 mm	12.5 mm	4 ul	1/4-20 UNC	New Item0	IDN7
6	12.7 mm	12.5 mm	4 ul	1/4-20 UNC	New Item0	IDN7
7	12.7 mm	19.05 mm	4 ul	1/4-20 UNC	New Item0	IDN7
8	12.7 mm	17.05 mm	4 ul	1/4-20 UNC	New Item0	IDN7
9	12.7 mm	19.05 mm	6 ul	1/4-20 UNC	New Item0	IDN7
10	12.7 mm	19.05 mm	6 ul	1/4-20 UNC	New Item0	IDN7

Figure 1–37

14. Click **OK** to close the iFeature Author dialog box.

15. Save and close **hole_array.ide**.

Task 3 - Insert the iFeature.

1. Open **drivenif.ipt**.

2. In the *Tools* tab>Options panel, click ⬚ (Application Options). Select the *iFeature* tab and verify that **Use Key 1 as Browser Name column** is enabled. By enabling this option, you can customize the name displayed in the Model browser for an iFeature to show the Key1 parameter name and its value. Click **OK**.

3. In the *Manage* tab>Insert panel, click 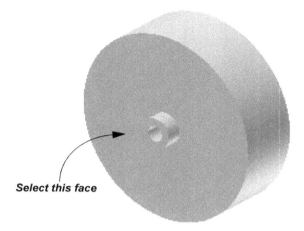 (Insert iFeature) or use the menu below this option to open **hole_array.ide**.

4. Select the face shown in Figure 1–38 as the position plane. Select the Axis row and select one of the cylinders as **Axis1**. A checkmark displays to the left of the name of the feature or sketch when the placement has been fully defined.

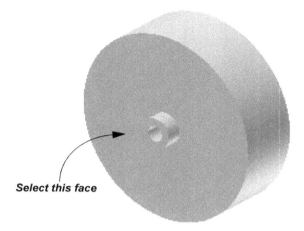

Select this face

Figure 1–38

5. Once you define the position, click **Next** to move to the Size step.

6. Accept the defaults in the *Size* area. Click **Next** to move to the Precise Pos. step.

7. Select **Do not Activate Sketch Edit**.

8. Click **Finish** to complete the operation.

As of the release of this material (March 2016), the addition of the iFeature was causing a failure. When the iFeature is initially displayed it is unexpectedly snapping to the central axis of the part. To resolve this issue the following workaround has been found. Keep in mind that the preview of the iFeature placement is not always the same as the actual geometry placement. You can always make changes to its position once it is placed.

9. Cancel the iFeature placement in the failure dialog box.

10. In the *Manage* tab>Insert panel, click **Insert iFeature** ( ) or use the menu below this option to open **hole_array.ide**.

11. Select the same face (Figure 1–38) as the position plane.

12. Select the Axis row and select one of the cylinders as **Axis1**. A checkmark displays to the left of the name of the feature or sketch when placement has been fully defined.

13. Select the Move grip that is positioned on the central axis and drag the iFeature away and place it away from the central axis, while still remaining on the geometry.

14. Once you define the position, click **Next**.

15. Accept the defaults in the *Size* area. Click **Next**.

16. Select **Do not Activate Sketch Edit**.

17. Click **Finish** to complete the operation. The model displays similar to that shown in Figure 1–39. The circle diameter is dependent on where you placed the Move grip. You can edit the feature and add dimensions to place the holes as required.

Figure 1–39

18. In the Model browser, expand the iFeature, right-click on the table, and select **Edit iFeature**. The Insert iFeature dialog box opens.

19. Enter new hole values, as shown in Figure 1–40.

20. Select the *Mating Assembly* value and enter **MCP0813** (shown in Figure 1–40) so that when the component is placed in an assembly, the mating component is identified.

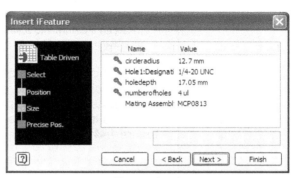

Figure 1–40

21. Click **Finish** to complete the operation. The model displays with four holes.

22. In the Model browser, right-click on **drivenif.ipt** and select **iProperties**. Select the *Custom* tab. Note that *Internal Drill Number* is listed as a custom property. Close the iProperties dialog box.

23. Save and close the model.

Practice 1c

Slotted Hole iFeature (Optional)

Practice Objectives

- Create an iFeature ensuring that all of the required geometry is included in the iFeature for accurate placement.
- Insert an iFeature into a new part file and vary the dimensional sizes to produce a required result.

In this practice, you will create an iFeature of a slotted hole. When placing the iFeature you will vary its angle and size. Minimal instructions are provided. Refer to the material for iFeatures if required. The completed model is shown in Figure 1–41.

Figure 1–41

Task 1 - Create a part with a slotted hole.

1. Create a new part based on the **Standard (in).ipt** template. Create the part as a ½" thick plate measuring 12" x 12", as shown in Figure 1–42.

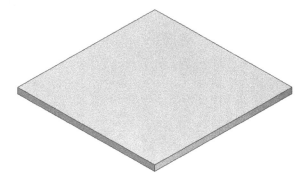

Figure 1–42

2. Start a new sketch on one of the large faces of the plate and randomly place six points using the $-\!\!\!+\!\!\!-$ (Point) option. It is not required to constrain or dimension these points. Finish the sketch. The model displays similar to that shown in Figure 1–43.

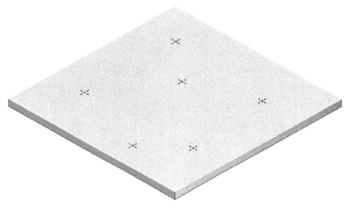

Figure 1–43

3. Start a new sketch on the same face as the sketch from Step 2. Do not just edit the previous sketch. Use the **Project Geometry** tool to project a point created in Step 2, as shown in Figure 1–44.

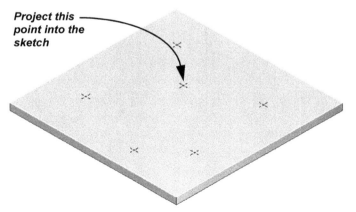

Project this point into the sketch

Figure 1–44

4. Sketch a slot, similar to that shown in Figure 1–45. Constrain the projected point to the midpoint of the center-to-center line. When editing the two values, enter **Slot_Length=3** and **Slot_Radius=.5** to rename the parameters, while at the same time editing the values of the parameters.

Renaming parameters while you are editing their values prevents you from having to open the Parameters dialog box to reassign names.

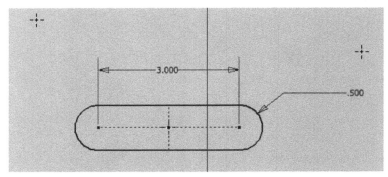

Figure 1–45

5. Finish the sketch.

6. Create the slot shown in Figure 1–46 using **Extrude**. Extrude the slot through **All** of the model.

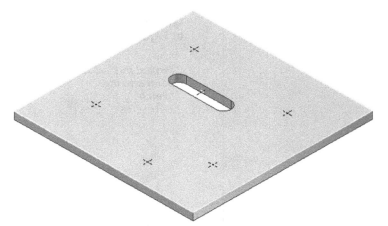

Figure 1–46

Task 2 - Create an iFeature.

1. In the *Manage* tab>Author panel, click 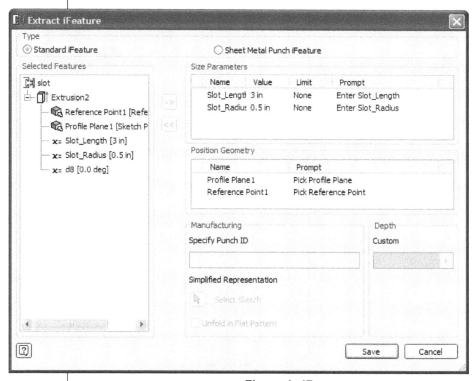 (Extract iFeature) to open the Extract iFeature dialog box.

2. Select the extrude (slot) feature.

3. Because the point was used as a reference in the slot sketch, it is available as a reference for the slot iFeature. In the *Selected Features* area, select **Reference Point1** and transfer it to the right area to add the work point to the iFeature.

4. Reorder the *Position Geometry* by dragging **Profile Plane1** above **Reference Point1**. Edit the prompts, as shown in Figure 1–47.

5. In the *Selected Features* area, right-click on **iFeature#** and select **Rename**. Enter **slot** as the new name.

Figure 1–47

6. Save the iFeature to your *Catalog* folder as **slot.ide**.

Task 3 - Insert the iFeature.

In this task, you insert a number of instances of the slot.ide feature in the same model.

1. In the *Manage* tab>Insert panel, click ⬚ (Insert iFeature) or use the menu below this option to open **slot.ide**.

2. Select the profile plane and slot center points to place the slots, as shown in Figure 1–48. You will need to add separate features for each instance. To rotate the slot on the profile plane, in the Insert iFeature dialog box, enter an *Angle*. To vary the sizes, you need to enter new values for the radius and length, as required. Keep in mind that the preview of the iFeature placement is not always the same as the actual geometry placement. You can always make changes to its position once it is placed.

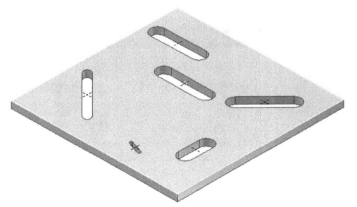

Figure 1–48

3. Save and close the model.

Chapter Review Questions

1. Renamed model parameters are automatically included as variable size parameters when creating an iFeature.

   a. True

   b. False

2. Which file extension type is used to store an iFeature?

   a. .IDW

   b. .IDE

   c. .IPN

   d. .IPT

3. Which of the following are valid menu options that can be used when defining limits on the parameter size of an iFeature? (Select all that apply.)

   a. Range

   b. List

   c. User Entry

   d. None

4. If you insert a revised iFeature into a file that contains an older version of the feature, the original iFeature is automatically updated.

   a. True

   b. False

5. Which of the following statements are true regarding the **Copy** option used to copy features. (Select all that apply.)

   a. It can only be used to copy features in the same model.

   b. It can be used to copy a chamfer from one edge and duplicate it on another edge.

   c. It can be used to create a copy of a sketched extrusion.

   d. A copied feature can always be created independent of the original; however, there are restrictions on when a dependent copy is possible.

6. Which of the following statements are true regarding the table-driven iFeatures? (Select all that apply.)

   a. The table for a table-driven iFeature is created during iFeature creation in a part model.

   b. All parameters defined during iFeature creation are automatically added as columns in the iFeature's table.

   c. The *Other* tab in the iFeature Author enables you to add iProperties to the table.

   d. Custom columns can be added in the iFeature Author and add a unique attribute value for each instance.

Command Summary

Button	Command	Location
	**Change Icon**	• **Ribbon:** *iFeature* tab>iFeature panel
N/A	**Copy** (features)	• **Context menu:** In Model browser with feature name selected
	Edit iFeature	• **Ribbon:** *iFeature* tab>iFeature panel • **Context menu** from the Model browser
	Edit Using Spread Sheet	• **Ribbon:** *iFeature* tab>iFeature panel
	Extract iFeature	• **Ribbon:** *Manage* tab>Author panel
	iFeature Author Table	• **Ribbon:** *iFeature* tab>iFeature panel • **Context menu:** In the graphics window
	Insert iFeature	• **Ribbon:** *Manage* tab>Insert panel
	Insert Object	• **Ribbon:** *Tools* tab>Insert panel
	View Catalog	• **Ribbon:** *iFeature* tab>iFeature panel

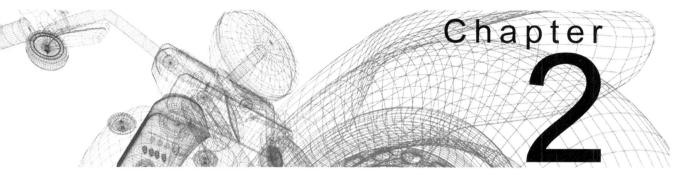

Chapter

2

iParts

The Autodesk® Inventor® iPart option is a design option that enables you to create variations in your part designs quickly and easily. iParts can be used to create similar models, instead of recreating the same model repeatably with slight variations. Once a part has been created with iPart members, the members can also be documented in a drawing using tables.

Learning Objectives in this Chapter

- Create an iPart that can generate different configurations of a model.
- Group iPart attributes into keys to logically sort the members for quick access to the configurations.
- Insert standard or custom iParts into an assembly based on specified Keys, Tree, or Table lists for the iPart factory.
- Replace an iPart in an assembly with a new iPart instance.
- Modify an iPart factory using the Edit Table or Edit via Spreadsheet options to add or modify parameters and attributes.
- Specify whether an edit made to an iPart should reflect only in the active member or in all members.
- Use a table-driven iPart to create an iFeature.
- Use a drawing table to clearly document the members and attributes that make up an iPart.

2.1 iPart Creation

Many similar parts are used in creating assemblies. For example, one bolt may differ from another bolt only in its length. Rather than create several bolts that are identical in all ways but length, you can create one iPart to cover all lengths. Like other part files, iPart files have the extension .IPT. The iPart in Figure 2–1 shows three configurations of a cover plate.

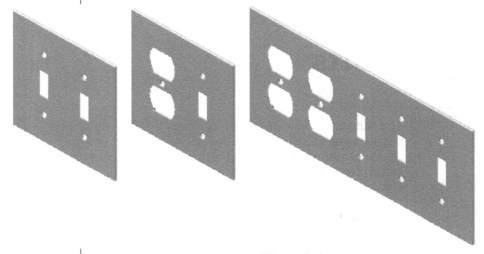

Figure 2–1

iPart files are called iPart Factories. The factory produces parts based on the part geometry and attribute values stored in a table. The new parts created by an iPart factory are unique files. By default, a part file is not created until the iPart is placed in an assembly.

General Steps

Use the following general steps to create an iPart:

1. Create or open a part with parameters.
2. Start the creation of an iPart.
3. Select the configurable attributes.
4. Verify the table.
5. Set up keys.
6. (Optional) Assign custom parameters.
7. Complete the operation.
8. Verify iPart instances in the Model browser.
9. (Optional) Generate iPart Members.

Step 1 - Create or open a part with parameters.

Create or open a part. To make it easier to create the iPart, use parameters that have descriptive names and apply those parameters to items in the features that will become your attributes. Consider the following:

* Plan your iPart so that a minimum number of parameters are required. If a dimension is always half of another dimension, use an equation rather than input both numbers.

* Consider what design variations are required and can be created. The parameters and dimensions that control this are used to create the iPart.

Step 2 - Start the creation of an iPart.

In the *Manage* tab>Author panel, click $\boxed{i}$ (Create iPart). The iPart Author dialog box opens, as shown in Figure 2–2.

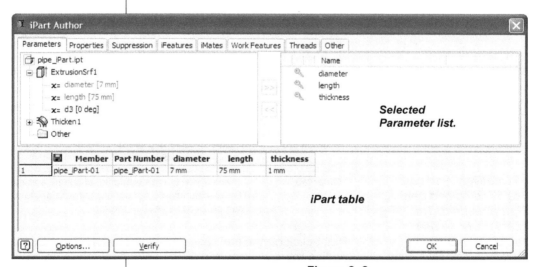

Figure 2–2

Step 3 - Select the configurable attributes.

The tabs in the iPart Author dialog box contain the configurable attributes that can be varied to create the different iPart configurations. Any parameter that has been renamed is automatically added as a configurable attribute. Use the $\boxed{>>}$ and $\boxed{<<}$ buttons to add and remove additional parameters, as required.

The iPart Author tabs are described as follows:

Tabs	Description
Parameters tab	Contains the parameters used in the part, which are listed under the features in which they belong.
Properties tab	Enables you to add feature information, such as the part number or the name of the manufacturer.
Suppression tab	Enables you to specify individual features to compute or suppress for each instance of the part.
iFeatures tab	Enables you to specify which table-driven instance of an iFeature to include in the iPart, or set the suppression status. Add the **Table Replace** item and assign rows from the iFeature to instances in the iPart.
iMates tab	Enables you to include iMates. You can specify to do any of the following: include, suppress, set offset values, specify matching name, and specify sequence number.
Work Features tab	Enables you to specify work features to include.
Threads tab	Enables you to add thread variables to the iPart. Designations such as UNC are case-sensitive.
Other tab	Enables you to create additional columns in the table. These columns do not control the size of the part, but can be used as keys in the table.

*Alternatively, you can use Excel to add new iPart members. This enables you to use some of the built-in Excel functionality, such as copy, paste, formulas, and sorting. To do so, click **OK**, right-click on Table in the Model browser, and select **Edit via Spreadsheet**.*

Right-click on the first row, and select **Insert Row**. Continue adding rows, as required. Each additional row is an additional iPart member or configuration.

The columns in the table shown in Figure 2–3 list the parameter names and other attributes added from the tabs. Each row lists the values for one iPart instance. Select each table cell and enter the required attribute value.

	🖫	Member	Part Number	diameter	length	thickness
1		Pipe-7x75x1	Pipe-7x75x1	7 mm	75 mm	1 mm
2		Pipe-7x80x1	Pipe-7x80x1	7 mm	80 mm	1 mm
3		Pipe-7x85x1	Pipe-7x85x1	7 mm	85 mm	1 mm
4		Pipe-7x75x1_1	Pipe-7x75x1_1	7 mm	75 mm	1.1 mm
5		Pipe-7x80x1_1	Pipe-7x80x1_1	7 mm	80 mm	1.1 mm
6		Pipe-7x85x1_1	Pipe-7x85x1_1	7 mm	85 mm	1.1 mm
7		Pipe-8x75x1	Pipe-8x75x1	8 mm	75 mm	1 mm
8		Pipe-8x80x1	Pipe-8x80x1	8 mm	80 mm	1 mm
9		Pipe-8x85x1	Pipe-8x85x1	8 mm	85 mm	1 mm
10		Pipe-8x75x1_1	Pipe-8x75x1_1	8 mm	75 mm	1.1 mm
11		Pipe-8x80x1_1	Pipe-8x80x1_1	8 mm	80 mm	1.1 mm
12		Pipe-8x85x1_1	Pipe-8x85x1_1	8 mm	85 mm	1.1 mm

Figure 2–3

- The row highlighted in green is the default part used when placing the iPart in an assembly. To change the default row, right-click on the required row and select **Set As Default Row**.

- To suppress a feature in a part, enter one of the following in the *iPart* table cell: Suppress, S, s, Off, OFF, off, 0.

- To compute the feature, enter one of the following in the cell: Compute, C, c, U, u, ON, on, On, 1.

- When entering values that require either **Exclude** or **Include**, the first letter in each word can be entered as lowercase, but the entire word is required to be a valid entry.

Step 4 - Verify the table.

To ensure all entered values are valid, click **Verify**. Invalid values highlight in the table in yellow. Correct all invalid values before continuing.

Step 5 - Set up keys.

Keys enable you to group iPart members according to their attribute values in a hierarchical manner. This sorts the iPart members logically, enabling quicker access to the required configuration.

If you do not assign keys, it can be much more difficult to find a specific configuration. Without creating any keys, configurations are listed as follows:

In the...	The configurations are listed...
iPart table	According to the order of the columns in the iPart table, as shown in Figure 2–4.
Model browser	According to the member name, as shown in Figure 2–5.
Place Standard iPart dialog box	Separately at the top-level branch, as shown in Figure 2–6.

	Member	Part Number	diameter	length	thickness
1	Pipe-7x75x1	Pipe-7x75x1	7 mm	75 mm	1 mm
2	Pipe-7x80x1	Pipe-7x80x1	7 mm	80 mm	1 mm
3	Pipe-7x85x1	Pipe-7x85x1	7 mm	85 mm	1 mm
4	Pipe-7x75x1_1	Pipe-7x75x1_1	7 mm	75 mm	1.1 mm
5	Pipe-7x80x1_1	Pipe-7x80x1_1	7 mm	80 mm	1.1 mm
6	Pipe-7x85x1_1	Pipe-7x85x1_1	7 mm	85 mm	1.1 mm
7	Pipe-8x75x1	Pipe-8x75x1	8 mm	75 mm	1 mm
8	Pipe-8x80x1	Pipe-8x80x1	8 mm	80 mm	1 mm
9	Pipe-8x85x1	Pipe-8x85x1	8 mm	85 mm	1 mm
10	Pipe-8x75x1_1	Pipe-8x75x1_1	8 mm	75 mm	1.1 mm
11	Pipe-8x80x1_1	Pipe-8x80x1_1	8 mm	80 mm	1.1 mm
12	Pipe-8x85x1_1	Pipe-8x85x1_1	8 mm	85 mm	1.1 mm

Figure 2–4

Figure 2–5

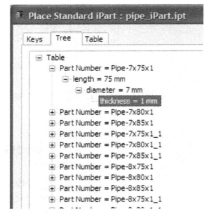

Figure 2–6

By assigning keys, you are able to organize these configurations into a logical and hierarchical structure, as shown in Figure 2–7. In the example shown, the iParts have been assigned keys for their diameter and thickness. This enables you to quickly expand the branches to find a required configuration, or easily view all of the different lengths that are available for a specific diameter and thickness.

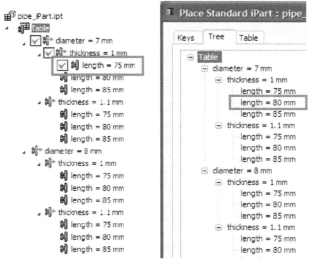

Figure 2–7

Not all attributes need keys. If assigned keys already narrow down the configurations to one, then no remaining keys are required.

To organize in this way you specify keys when you create the iPart factory. A key symbol displays in front of each parameter, as shown in Figure 2–8.

- Blue keys indicate that the attribute is set as a key.

- Gray keys indicate that the attribute is not used as a key.

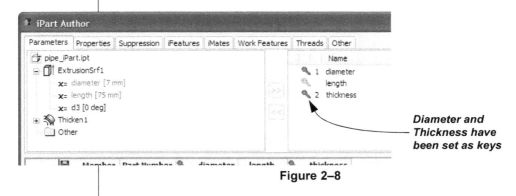

Diameter and Thickness have been set as keys

Figure 2–8

- The number next to the key indicates the hierarchy: 1 is the first key used for sorting, followed by 2, etc. Use the most descriptive or logical attribute as the first key.

- Up to nine keys can be used in a part factory. Click on a key to toggle it on or off.

- To change the order of key numbers, or to assign a key number to a parameter, in the *Name* column or table, right-click on the parameter and select **Key**. Select the required key number, as shown in Figure 2–9. You can also select a key to assign it to the next non-assigned key value.

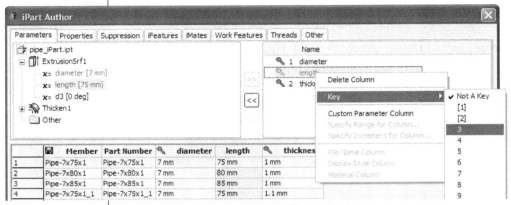

Figure 2–9

Step 6 - (Optional) Assign custom parameters.

A keyed column cannot be set as a custom column.

Parameters can be set up so that when you are placing the iPart factory member in an assembly, you are prompted to enter its value. When a custom parameter is assigned, the iPart is considered a custom iPart.

To assign a custom parameter, right-click on the parameter's heading and select **Custom Parameter Column**, as shown in Figure 2–10. Once assigned, the entire column turns blue, indicating that it is custom. It can be disabled later, if required, by clearing the **Custom Parameter Column** option.

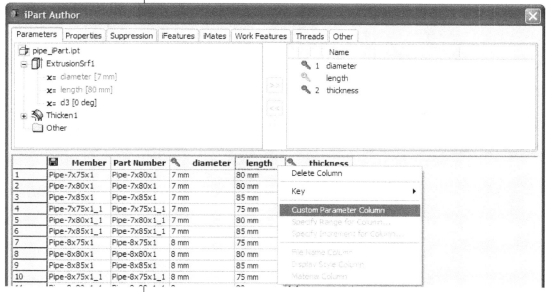

Figure 2–10

Step 7 - Complete the operation.

Once the iPart is defined, click **OK** to complete iPart creation.

Step 8 - Verify iPart instances in the Model browser.

After you have defined the iPart Factory, the table is listed in the Model browser. The members can be listed by their name or by key. Right-click on **Table** in the Model browser and select **List by Keys** or **List by Member Name** to customize the display of the members to either option.

Expand the table to see the configurations of the part defined in the table (organized according to the key attribute(s) you defined). The left side of Figure 2–11 shows the members displayed by key. The member name display is shown on the right side.

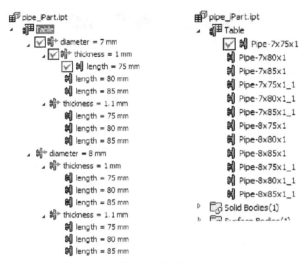

Figure 2–11

The active iPart member is marked with a checkmark. Double-click on the most-nested branches to activate that configuration (or right-click and select **Activate**). The most-nested branches are not expandable (i.e., an arrowhead symbol does not exist next to it in the Model browser).

Step 9 - (Optional) Generate iPart Members.

Once the iPart is created, you can create the member when it is used in an assembly or you can generate all the files at once.

How To: Generate All the Files at Once

1. In the Model browser, right-click on **Table** and select **List By Member Name**.
2. Hold <Shift> and select all member names.
3. Right-click and select **Generate Files**, as shown in Figure 2–12.

*If you selected **List By Keys**, you must select the most nested member names.*

Figure 2–12

If a Custom Parameter column is specified in the table, you will not be able to generate files. This is because the parameter is a required entry when the component is placed in an assembly; therefore, generating the files does not prompt you for user entry.

The iPart members are created in a folder with the same name as the iPart file. In the above example, a folder called *hex_bolt* was created and contains four files.

2.2 iPart Placement

Inserting iParts in assemblies is similar to inserting parts, except you must specify a member to use. The procedure varies depending on if they are a standard factory (does not contain any custom cells) or from a custom iPart factory (contains at least one custom cell).

When selecting iPart members for placement, the three tabs provide different ways of listing the same iPart members. This helps you quickly find the part you are looking for.

- The *Keys* tab, as shown in Figure 2–13, lists members in the order specified in the iPart Factory along with their current values. Click on a value to select a different standard value or to change a custom value. After the value for one attribute is selected, only the valid corresponding values will be listed for the other attributes.

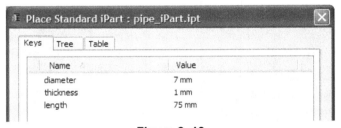

Figure 2–13

- The *Tree* tab, as shown in Figure 2–14, lists the values for each instance of the iPart. Expand the tree to see and select the instances of the part defined in the table (organized according to the key attribute[s]).

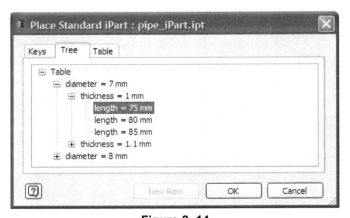

Figure 2–14

- The *Table* tab, as shown in Figure 2–15, lists the values for each instance of the iPart in the iPart Factory. Right-click on a column header to select ascending or descending sort order.

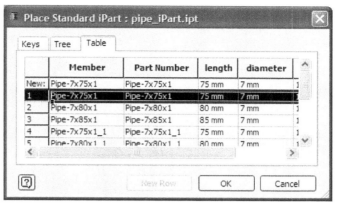

Figure 2–15

Placing a Standard iPart

How To: Place a Standard iPart

1. In the *Assemble* tab>Component panel, click (Place).
2. Select and open the iPart. The Place Standard iPart dialog box opens.
3. Select an iPart member using one of the following methods:
   - Select the current value in the *Keys* tab.
   - Select an instance from the *Tree* tab.
   - Select a row in the *Table* tab.

4. Select a point on the screen to place the component.
5. Repeat Steps 1 to 3 to place any additional iPart members.
6. Right-click and select **OK**.
7. Constrain the component in the assembly, as required.

When you place a standard iPart for the first time, the Autodesk Inventor software creates a new directory in the same directory as the iPart factory. The directory is created using the same name as the iPart factory. As you place iParts from the factory, each part is created and it is added to the folder.

Placing a custom iPart

How To: Place a Custom iPart

1. In the *Assemble* tab>Component panel, click 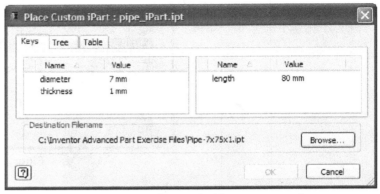 (Place).
2. Select and open the iPart. The Place Custom iPart dialog box opens as shown in Figure 2–16. The right column contains the values you can customize.

Figure 2–16

3. Select an iPart member using one of the following methods:
   - Select the current value in the *Keys* tab.
   - Select an instance from the *Tree* tab.
   - Select a row in the *Table* tab.

4. Set the values for the custom items as required.
5. (Optional) Click **Browse** to change the *Destination Filename* for the new part. Standard iParts are named by default.
6. Select a point on the screen to place the component.
7. Right-click and select **OK**.
8. Constrain the component in the assembly, as required

Replacing an iPart

How To: Replace iPart Components

1. In the Model browser, expand the component, right-click on the **Table** node and select **Change Component**.
2. Select the new iPart instance to use.
3. Click **OK** to replace the instance.

2.3 Editing an iPart Factory

Edit Table

How To: Edit the iPart factory

1. Open the iPart factory as you would open any part file.
2. In the Model browser, right-click on the **Table** node in the Model browser and select **Edit Table** to open the iPart Author dialog box.
3. Add or change the entries in the dialog box, and click **OK**.
4. Save the changes to the file.

Changes that are made to an iPart Factory reflect in the iPart instances already placed in assemblies once their assembly has been updated.

Alternatively, in the Model browser, right-click on the **Table** node in the Model browser and select **Edit via Spreadsheet** to access the spreadsheet in Excel. You can add equations and relate the cells to each other. Equations that are entered in Excel display in red and cannot be changed in the iPart Author dialog box.

Adding Features to an iPart

When adding features to an existing iPart, considering the scope of the change is important. Consider whether the new feature should reflect in only the active factory member (**Edit Member Scope**) or reflect in all factory members (**Edit Factory Scope**). In the Author panel, the **Edit Member Scope** and **Edit Factory Scope** options, as shown in Figure 2–17, enable you to control the scope of change.

Figure 2–17

- By default, the scope is automatically set to change the entire factory (**Edit Factory Scope**), which means that if a feature is added, it is added to all members and no changes are made to the iPart table.

- If **Edit Member Scope** is specified and a feature is added, the feature and any dimensional parameters used to create it are automatically added to the table. The feature's cell for the active member will be marked to "Compute". Other members are automatically "Suppressed", but can be modified if required.

2.4 Creating iFeatures from a Table-Driven iPart

The entire table of data for the iPart is included in the new iFeature. You do not need to manually enter all instances of the iPart into the table.

Table-driven iParts, in their entirety, can be used to create a table-driven iFeature. This enables you to create an iFeature directly from a whole table-driven iPart.

How To: Create a Table-driven iFeature from a Table-driven iPart

1. Create a table-driven iPart using the standard workflow.
2. In the *Manage* tab>Author panel, click 🔲 (Extract iFeature). The Extract iFeature dialog box opens.
3. In the Model browser, select the required features, or select those directly from the model geometry. To select the entire iPart, select the base feature first, and all following features will automatically be selected. Assign any of the *Size Parameters* or *Position Geometry*, as shown in Figure 2–18.

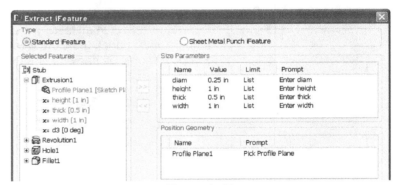

Figure 2–18

4. Save the iFeature in the catalog directory. The iFeature can be placed using the same techniques as placing any iFeature.

2.5 Tables for Factory Members

You can create tables for iParts and iAssemblies to show factory members and their attributes, as shown in Figure 2–19.

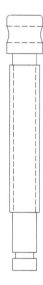

Table		
Member	Part Number	vise_screw_length
Short	Vise_Screw-01	138.75 mm
Medium	Vise_Screw-02	158.75 mm
Long	Vise_Screw-03	178.75 mm

Figure 2–19

How To: Create a Table for iPart Factory Members

1. Open or create a drawing that contains a view of an iPart member.
2. Select the *Annotate* tab>Table panel and click ⊞ (General). The Table dialog box opens.
3. Select a drawing view containing the required iPart for which you want to create a table. The Table dialog box updates, as shown in Figure 2–20.

Figure 2–20

4. Click 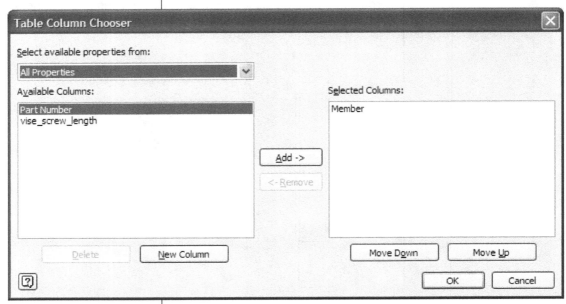 (Column Chooser). The Table Column Chooser dialog box opens, as shown in Figure 2–21.

Table Column Chooser

Select available properties from:

All Properties

Available Columns:

Part Number
vise_screw_length

Add ->

<- Remove

Selected Columns:

Member

Delete   New Column

Move Down   Move Up

OK   Cancel

Figure 2–21

5. Customize the columns that will be displayed in the table and click **OK**.

- Move the required column properties from the *Available Columns* list to the *Selected Columns* list to create it as a column in the table and display the attribute value for each factory member.
- You can reorder the column properties in the *Selected Columns* list as required by clicking **Move Down** and **Move Up**.

6. Click **OK** to close the Table dialog box.
7. Move the cursor to the required location and click to place the table. The table populates with the columns and attributes of the iPart factory members.

Practice 2a | Bolt iPart Factory

Practice Objectives

- Create an iPart factory using custom parameters to show different configurations of the part.
- Group iPart attributes into Keys to sort the iPart members logically, enabling quick access to the configuration.
- Add a new feature to the model and edit the member scope to define how the new feature will appear in the iPart.
- Generate the members of the iPart factory to create new part models.

In this practice, you rename part parameters so they have a descriptive name and are easily identifiable. You then establish logical relationships between these parameters so that only a small number of parameters control them all. Using these parameters you then create an iPart factory to quickly produce multiple bolt parts. The hex_bolt you will be working with is shown in Figure 2–22.

Figure 2–22

Task 1 - Change parameter names.

In this task, you change the bolt dimension (parameter) names to descriptive names. You also relate the parameters.

1. Open **hex_bolt.ipt**.

2. In the *Manage* tab>Parameters panel, click f_x (Parameters) and change the parameter names as follows:

- d0 = stub_len
- d6 = major_dia
- d7 = minor_dia
- d9 = h_width
- d10 = h_height
- d23 = thread_len
- d24 = grip_len

3. Enter the following equation for the thread_len parameter:

- thread_len = stub_len - grip_len

This equation calculates the length of the thread when the stub length is changed.

4. Close the Parameters dialog box.

Task 2 - Create an iPart factory.

1. In the *Manage* tab>Author panel, click 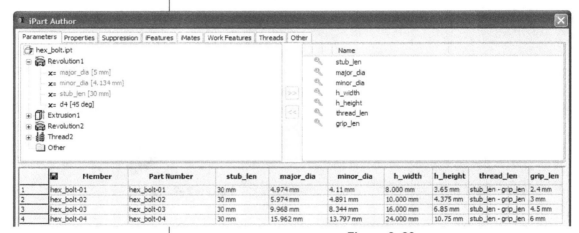 (Create iPart). The iPart Author dialog box opens. Note that the named parameters are already listed in the column on the right side and in the lower table.

2. Insert three more rows to the table by right-clicking on row **1** and selecting **Insert Row**. Enter the values shown in the Figure 2–23.

iPart Author

| Parameters | Properties | Suppression | iFeatures | iMates | Work Features | Threads | Other |

hex_bolt.ipt
- Revolution1
  - x= major_dia [5 mm]
  - x= minor_dia [4.134 mm]
  - x= stub_len [30 mm]
  - x= d4 [45 deg]
- Extrusion1
- Revolution2
- Thread2
- Other

Name
- stub_len
- major_dia
- minor_dia
- h_width
- h_height
- thread_len
- grip_len

	Member	Part Number	stub_len	major_dia	minor_dia	h_width	h_height	thread_len	grip_len
1	hex_bolt-01	hex_bolt-01	30 mm	4.974 mm	4.11 mm	8.000 mm	3.65 mm	stub_len - grip_len	2.4 mm
2	hex_bolt-02	hex_bolt-02	30 mm	5.974 mm	4.891 mm	10.000 mm	4.375 mm	stub_len - grip_len	3 mm
3	hex_bolt-03	hex_bolt-03	30 mm	9.968 mm	8.344 mm	16.000 mm	6.85 mm	stub_len - grip_len	4.5 mm
4	hex_bolt-04	hex_bolt-04	30 mm	15.962 mm	13.797 mm	24.000 mm	10.75 mm	stub_len - grip_len	6 mm

Figure 2–23

3. Select the *Threads* tab and add **Thread2:Designation** to the right column. The attribute is also added in the iPart table as a new column.

4. Enter the values shown in Figure 2–24 for the Thread Designation.

Member	Part Number	stub_len	major_dia	minor_dia	h_width	h_height	thread_len	grip_len	Thread2: Designation
hex_bolt-01	hex_bolt-01	30 mm	4.974 mm	4.11 mm	8.000 mm	3.65 mm	stub_len - grip_len	2.4 mm	M5x0.8
hex_bolt-02	hex_bolt-02	30 mm	5.974 mm	4.891 mm	10.000 mm	4.375 mm	stub_len - grip_len	3 mm	M6x1
hex_bolt-03	hex_bolt-03	30 mm	9.968 mm	8.344 mm	16.000 mm	6.85 mm	stub_len - grip_len	4.5 mm	M10x1.5
hex_bolt-04	hex_bolt-04	30 mm	15.962 mm	13.797 mm	24.000 mm	10.75 mm	stub_len - grip_len	6 mm	M16x2

Figure 2–24

Task 3 - Assign keys.

1. In the *Threads* tab, next to **Thread2:Designation**, click 🔑 to assign it as Key 1. The key turns blue.

2. Assign Keys 2 and 3 to **stub_len** and **major_dia**, consecutively.

3. Click **OK** to close the iPart Author dialog box.

*If the Model browser is already displayed by keys, **List by Keys** will not be available.*

4. In Model browser, expand the Table. To configure the Model browser to display the iPart configurations listed by keys, right-click on Table and select **List by Keys**. Expand the branches for the first thread designation, as shown in Figure 2–25.

Figure 2–25

*If your iPart table is created with recognizable part numbers as the Member name you might want to consider setting the Table to **List by Member Name** so you can easily activate a member of the iPart family.*

5. To activate another iPart configuration, expand it in the Model browser until it cannot expand further and double-click on the last key describing the configuration. This single iPart can be used in assemblies to add different configurations of the bolt.

The Autodesk Inventor software enables you to create an iFeature from an iPart if the design intent exists.

6. Save the model.

Task 4 - Add a feature to the iPart.

1. Review the panel and note that the 📝 (Edit Factory Scope) is enabled. This is the default option, as shown in Figure 2–26.

Figure 2–26

2. Create a cut feature similar to that shown in Figure 2–27 on the active factory member.

Create this cut with the Edit Factory Scope option set

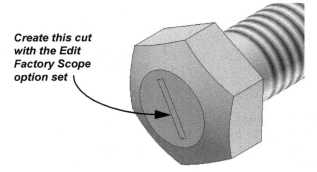

Figure 2–27

3. In the Model browser, right-click on **Table** and select **List By Member Name**.

4. Double-click on the three other factory members to verify that this feature has been added to all members. If the values for the cut must be varied for each member, use the standard editing tools to add the parameters and modify them in the table.

5. Activate **hex_bolt-01**.

6. In the *Manage* tab>Author panel, click 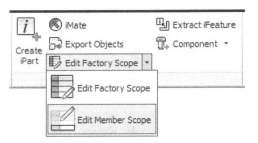 (Edit Member Scope), as shown in Figure 2–28.

Figure 2–28

Consider setting up equations to ensure that the dimensions of both cuts are the same, or use sketching techniques to build both sketches into a single sketch but use it to create two extrusions.

7. Create a cut feature similar to that shown in Figure 2–29. For this practice, use similar dimensions to those used to create the previous cut.

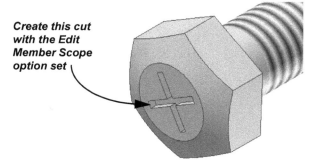

Create this cut with the Edit Member Scope option set

Figure 2–29

8. Double-click on the three other factory members to verify that this feature has not been added to the other members. It is only shown in the **hex_bolt-01** member because this was the active member when the feature was created.

9. Activate **hex_bolt-01**.

10. Right-click on Table in the Model browser and select **Edit Table** to open the iPart Author dialog box.

11. Note the new column shown in Figure 2–30. Note that Suppress is enabled for the cut in **hex_bolt-02**, **hex_bolt-03**, and h**ex_bolt-04**, and the cut is computed in **hex_bolt-01**. The Suppression/Compute setting can be modified, if required. The values of the sketch dimensions can also be added to the table, if required, to control the size of the cuts in each factory instance.

eight	thread_len	grip_len	🖉	Thread2: Designation	Extrusion3
mm	stub_len - grip_len	2.4 mm		M5x0.8	Compute
5 mm	stub_len - grip_len	3 mm		M6x1	Suppress
mm	stub_len - grip_len	4.5 mm		M10x1.5	Suppress
5 mm	stub_len - grip_len	6 mm		M16x2	Suppress

Figure 2–30

12. Close the iPart Author dialog box.

Task 5 - Generate the members of the factory.

1. Verify that the Model browser is still set to **List By Member Name**.

2. Hold <Shift> and select all four member names.

3. Right-click and select **Generate Files**, as shown in Figure 2–31.

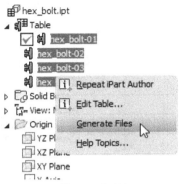

Figure 2–31

4. If you did not previously save the iPart file, you are prompted to save the file prior to file generation. Open Windows Explorer and review the four files in the new *Hex_Bolt* folder in the practice files directory.

5. Return to the Autodesk Inventor software.

Task 6 - Assign a custom parameter.

Although values have been assigned to the *grip_len* parameter for each iPart member, the values might need to vary depending on the current requirements when the hex_bolt is placed in an assembly. In this case, the column will be set as custom. The default values that were provided in the table will be used; however, designers will still have the option to enter custom values, if required.

1. In the Model browser, right-click on **Table** and select **Edit Table**. The iPart Author dialog box opens.

2. Right-click on the *grip_len* column header and select **Custom Parameter Column**, as shown in Figure 2–32. The column will turn blue, indicating that it is a custom column.

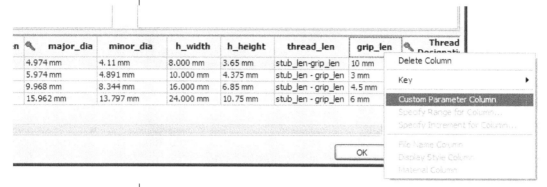

n	major_dia	minor_dia	h_width	h_height	thread_len	grip_len	Thread Designati...
	4.974 mm	4.11 mm	8.000 mm	3.65 mm	stub_len-grip_len	10 mm	Delete Column
	5.974 mm	4.891 mm	10.000 mm	4.375 mm	stub_len - grip_len	3 mm	Key ▶
	9.968 mm	8.344 mm	16.000 mm	6.85 mm	stub_len - grip_len	4.5 mm	Custom Parameter Column
	15.962 mm	13.797 mm	24.000 mm	10.75 mm	stub_len - grip_len	6 mm	Specify Range for Column...
							Specify Increment for Column...
						OK	File Name Column
							Display Style Column
							Material Column

Figure 2–32

3. Click **OK** to close the iPart Author dialog box.

If a Custom Parameter Column is specified in the table, you are not able to generate files using the **Generate Files** command. You can only generate files when the part is assembled. This is because the parameter is a required entry when the component is placed in an assembly, and using the **Generate Files** command does not prompt you for user entry.

4. The iPart factory is ready to be placed. Save the file with the name **hex_bolt_iPart** and close the window.

Practice 2b

Create an iPart Factory

Practice Objectives

- Create an iPart factory using user parameters to show different configurations of the part.
- Modify and edit the iPart factory parameters and attributes in Autodesk Inventor software and Microsoft Excel.
- Place an iPart into an assembly file.
- Replace an iPart component in an assembly file with another instance from its factory.

In this practice, you create two user-defined parameters for a light-switch cover and assign them to part dimensions. To sort the instances of the part, you create an iPart factory to produce cover parts for varying combinations of switches and jacks. You edit the cover part and add a new row and column to the iPart factory via a spreadsheet. Finally, you place and constrain one instance in an assembly file. The final assembly is shown in Figure 2–33.

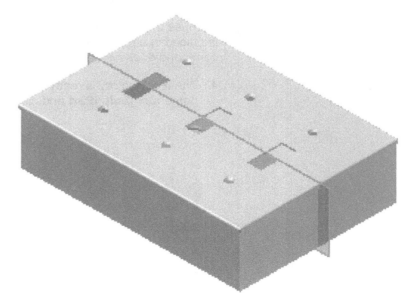

Figure 2–33

Task 1 - Create user-defined parameters.

In this task, you create two user-defined parameters and assign these parameters to part dimensions to sort various instances of the cover part.

1. Open **cover.ipt**. The model displays as shown in Figure 2–34.

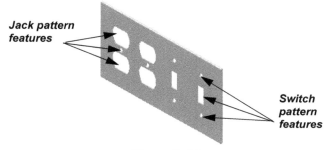

Figure 2–34

2. Use the Model browser to examine the cover part features and pattern numbers for the switch and jack pattern features.

3. In the *Manage* tab>Parameters panel, click f_x (Parameters). The Parameters dialog box opens.

4. Click **Add Numeric** and create two user-defined unitless (ul) parameters called **switches** and **jackpairs**, as shown in Figure 2–35.

d59	mm					
d60	mm	58.42 mm	58.420000	○	58.420000	☐
User Parameters						
switches	ul	2 ul	2.000000	○	2.000000	☐
jackpairs	ul	2 ul	2.000000	○	2.000000	☐

Figure 2–35

5. Change the equation for the d0 dimension to the following to make it equal to the overall length of the part:

   • 25.4+(45.72*(switches+jackpairs))

6. Change the equation for the d18 dimension to **switches**.

7. Change the equation for the d50 dimension to **jackpairs**. The d18 and d50 dimensions are pattern numbers for the switches and jackpairs in the cover part.

8. Click **Done** to close the Parameters dialog box.

9. Update the model, if required.

10. Show the dimensions for the **Extrusion1**. Change the dimension display to **Expression.** The model displays as shown in Figure 2–36.

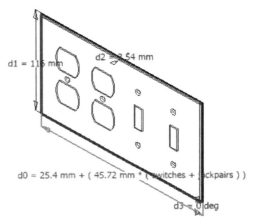

Figure 2–36

Task 2 - Create an iPart factory.

In this task, you create an iPart factory to sort the various instances of the cover part by pattern numbers for the switches and jackpairs.

1. Suppress the switch pattern and jack pattern features.

2. In the *Manage* tab>Author panel, click (Create iPart). The iPart Author dialog box opens. Note that the named parameters are already listed in the column on the right side of the table.

3. Select the key symbol next to the parameter switches in the right side panel. Key 1 is automatically assigned, the key turns blue, and a number 1 displays beside it.

4. Select the key symbol next to jackpairs to set it as Key 2. The key turns blue and a number 2 appears beside it.

5. Select the *Suppression* tab. The suppressed features are already listed in the column on the right side of the table.

6. Add **switch**, **switch holes**, **jacks**, and **jack holes** to the column on the right side. The features are also added as columns at the bottom of the table.

7. Right-click on row 1 and select **Insert Row**. Insert four more rows to the table and add the entries shown in Figure 2–37.

   - To suppress a feature in a part in the iPart table, enter one of the following entries in a cell: Suppress, S, s, Off, OFF, off, 0.

   - To compute the feature, enter one of the following entries in the cell: Compute, C, c, U, u, ON, on, On, 1.

	Member	Part Number	switches	jackpairs	switch pattern	jack pattern	switch	switch holes	jacks	jack holes
1	cover-01	cover-01	1 ul	3 ul	Suppress	Compute	Compute	Compute	Compute	Compute
2	cover-02	cover-02	2 ul	1 ul	Compute	Suppress	Compute	Compute	Compute	Compute
3	cover-03	cover-03	3 ul	0 ul	Compute	Suppress	Compute	Compute	Suppress	Suppress
4	cover-04	cover-04	1 ul	1 ul	Suppress	Suppress	Compute	Compute	Compute	Compute
5	cover-05	cover-05	0 ul	1 ul	Suppress	Suppress	Suppress	Suppress	Compute	Compute
6	cover-06	cover-06	3 ul	2 ul	Compute	Compute	Compute	Compute	Compute	Compute

Figure 2–37

8. Right-click on row 6 and select **Set As Default Row**.

9. Click **OK** to close the iPart Author dialog box. The cover part displays as shown in Figure 2–38. The features are computed according to the conditions you set in the table.

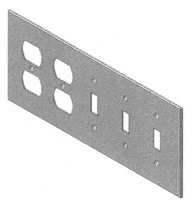

Figure 2–38

10. Save the model.

Task 3 - Edit the iPart factory.

1. Expand Table and ensure that the table display is as shown in Figure 2–39 showing all the keys not Model Names. If not, right-click on **Table** and select **List by Keys**. Expand **switches = 3**. The Model browser displays as shown in Figure 2–39.

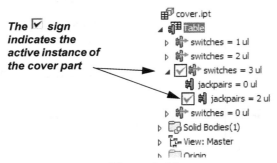

Figure 2–39

2. In the Model browser, expand **switches = 2 ul** and double-click on the **jackpairs = 1ul** node. The part displays as shown in Figure 2–40.

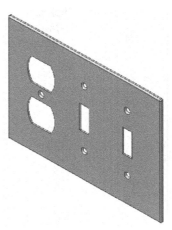

Figure 2–40

3. In the Model browser, right-click on **Table** and select **Edit Table**. The iPart Author dialog box opens.

4. Make row 3(cover-03) the default and click **OK**. The cover part displays as shown in Figure 2–41.

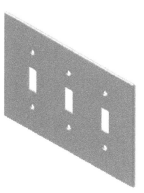

Figure 2–41

Task 4 - Edit the iPart factory via spreadsheet.

In this task, you add a row to the iPart table using a spreadsheet. You also add a column to the table to calculate the overall length of various instances.

1. In the Model browser, right-click on **Table** and select **Edit via Spreadsheet**. Click **OK** to confirm that the changes made via the Spreadsheet will take effect after the Excel process is closed.

2. Edit the iPart table in Microsoft Excel to remove the "ul" dimension from columns C and D, as shown in Figure 2–42.

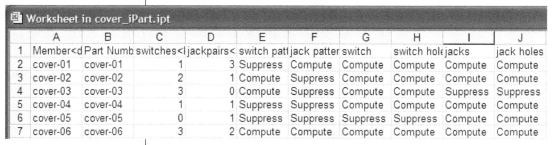

	A	B	C	D	E	F	G	H	I	J
1	Member<d	Part Numb	switches<l	jackpairs<	switch pat|	jack patter	switch	switch hol{	jacks	jack holes
2	cover-01	cover-01	1	3	Suppress	Compute	Compute	Compute	Compute	Compute
3	cover-02	cover-02	2	1	Compute	Suppress	Compute	Compute	Compute	Compute
4	cover-03	cover-03	3	0	Compute	Suppress	Compute	Compute	Suppress	Suppress
5	cover-04	cover-04	1	1	Suppress	Suppress	Compute	Compute	Compute	Compute
6	cover-05	cover-05	0	1	Suppress	Suppress	Suppress	Suppress	Compute	Compute
7	cover-06	cover-06	3	2	Compute	Compute	Compute	Compute	Compute	Compute

Figure 2–42

3. Add a row to the table with the values shown in Figure 2–43. The values are shown in row 8 of the table.

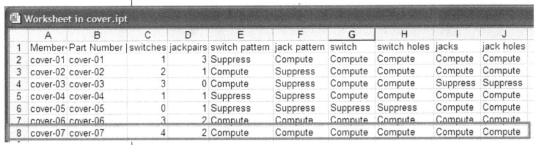

	A	B	C	D	E	F	G	H	I	J
	Member	Part Number	switches	jackpairs	switch pattern	jack pattern	switch	switch holes	jacks	jack holes
1										
2	cover-01	cover-01	1	3	Suppress	Compute	Compute	Compute	Compute	Compute
3	cover-02	cover-02	2	1	Compute	Suppress	Compute	Compute	Compute	Compute
4	cover-03	cover-03	3	0	Compute	Suppress	Compute	Compute	Suppress	Suppress
5	cover-04	cover-04	1	1	Suppress	Suppress	Compute	Compute	Compute	Compute
6	cover-05	cover-05	0	1	Suppress	Suppress	Suppress	Suppress	Compute	Compute
7	cover-06	cover-06	3	2	Compute	Compute	Compute	Compute	Compute	Compute
8	cover-07	cover-07	4	2	Compute	Compute	Compute	Compute	Compute	Compute

Figure 2–43

4. Save the Microsoft Excel file and close excel to return to cover.ipt.

5. Activate the new row. The cover part displays as shown in Figure 2–44.

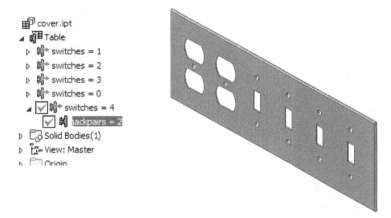

Figure 2–44

6. Open the iPart table using Microsoft Excel and add a column called **Overall Length** to the table.

7. Enter the formula below in each cell of the new column by replacing the "switches" and "jackpairs" with the corresponding C# and D#, as shown in Figure 2–45. Verify that none of the values under the switches and jackpairs columns contain "ul". The formula for the overall length is:

   • 25.4+(45.72*(switches+jackpairs))

The table displays as shown in Figure 2–45.

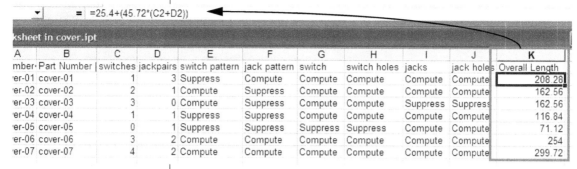

	$= 25.4+(45.72*(C2+D2))$									
xsheet in cover.ipt										
A	B	C	D	E	F	G	H	I	J	K
mber	Part Number	switches	jackpairs	switch pattern	jack pattern	switch	switch holes	jacks	jack holes	Overall Length
er-01	cover-01	1	3	Suppress	Compute	Compute	Compute	Compute	Compute	208.28
er-02	cover-02	2	1	Compute	Suppress	Compute	Compute	Compute	Compute	162.56
er-03	cover-03	3	0	Compute	Suppress	Compute	Compute	Suppress	Suppress	162.56
er-04	cover-04	1	1	Suppress	Suppress	Compute	Compute	Compute	Compute	116.84
er-05	cover-05	0	1	Suppress	Suppress	Suppress	Suppress	Compute	Compute	71.12
er-06	cover-06	3	2	Compute	Compute	Compute	Compute	Compute	Compute	254
er-07	cover-07	4	2	Compute	Compute	Compute	Compute	Compute	Compute	299.72

Figure 2–45

8. Save and close the Excel file and return to the part.

9. Edit the table. Note the color of the *Overall Length* column. Equations that are entered in Microsoft Excel cannot be changed in the iPart Author dialog box. Additionally, cells that contain these values display in red in the iPart Author dialog box.

10. Right-click the heading of the *Overall Length* column and select **Key>3** to assign Key 3 to the overall length column.

11. Make row 3 default. Close the dialog box.

12. In the Model browser, expand **Table** (change the Table to list by keys, if required). The overall length for each instance displays in the Model browser, as shown in Figure 2–46.

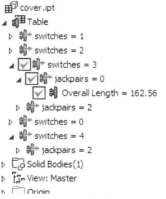

Figure 2–46

13. Save Copy As the part with the name **cover_iPart** and close the window. Do not save cover.ipt. This enables you to retain the original cover part.

Task 5 - Place the cover_iPart.

1. Create a new assembly file using the **Standard (mm).iam** template.

2. Place one instance of the **box_cover.ipt** part in the assembly. Right-click and select **Place Grounded at Origin** to place the first file in the assembly at (0, 0, 0).

3. In the *Assemble* tab>Component panel, click 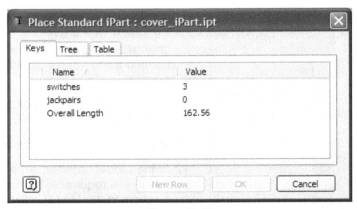 (Place) and select and open the **cover_iPart.ipt** Component. The Place Standard iPart dialog box opens, as shown in Figure 2–47, showing the default key parameter values you previously set.

Figure 2–47

4. Select a point on the screen, right-click and select **OK**.

5. When you place a standard iPart for the first time, the Autodesk Inventor software creates a new directory in the same directory as the iPart factory. The directory is created using the same name as the iPart factory. As you place iParts from the factory, each part is created and is added to the folder. Open Windows Explorer and review the folder called *cover_iPart* in the practice files directory.

6. Fully constrain the cover_iPart. The assembly displays as shown in Figure 2–48.

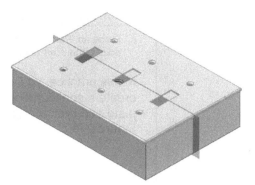

Figure 2–48

Task 6 - Change the cover-03 component in the assembly.

1. In the Model browser, expand **cover-03**, right-click on **Table** and select **Change Component**. The Place Standard iPart dialog box opens.

You can select iPart factory components to use in an assembly using any of the three tabs; Keys, Tree, and Table. In this situation it was easier to review the table for the correct length and select the required configuration.

2. The only other component that will fit with the current size of the box_cover is **cover-02**. Select the *Table* tab, select **cover-02** (row 2) and click **OK**. The assembly displays as shown in Figure 2–49.

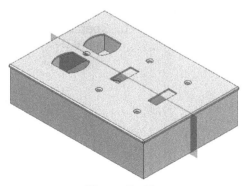

Figure 2–49

To further automate this assembly, you can design it using Adaptivity or iAssemblies so that selecting a different cover_iPart causes an update in the cover_box.

3. Save the assembly as **assembly_iPart** and close the window.

Practice 2c

iParts in Assemblies

Practice Objective

- Place an iPart into an assembly by modifying a custom parameter and editing the iPart to include a new configuration.

In this practice, you modify an iPart table in the hex-bolt part to create a configuration that can be used in an assembly with the plate and switch covers. The final assembly is shown in Figure 2–50.

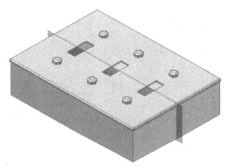

Figure 2–50

Task 1 - Open an assembly file and measure the diameter of a hole.

1. Open **outlet.iam**. The model displays as shown in Figure 2–51.

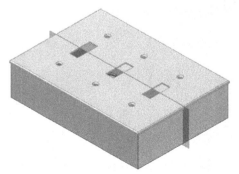

Figure 2–51

2. Measure the diameter of a hole in the cover component. This value will be used to create a new entry in the **hex_bolt_ipart_final.ipt** that fit the holes.

Task 2 - Create a new entry for the hex_bolt to fit the assembly.

1. Open **hex_bolt_ipart_final.ipt**.

2. Add an entry of **M5x0.8** to the Designation with a diameter that can be used in the assembly. Verify that the configuration can be generated and opens.

3. Place **hex_bolt_ipart_final** into the outlet assembly using the configuration that you just created. The Place Custom iPart dialog box opens, enabling you to enter a custom value for the **grip_len** parameter. This parameter was set as a custom parameter in the iPart file. Click in the *Value* cell beside **grip_len** and enter **3** as the custom value, as shown in Figure 2–52. Select the appropriate **major_dia** for the hole.

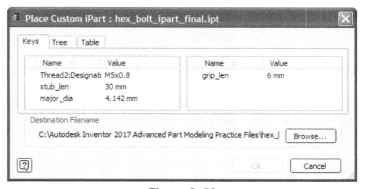

Figure 2–52

4. Assemble the remaining five bolts. The final assembly displays as shown in Figure 2–53.

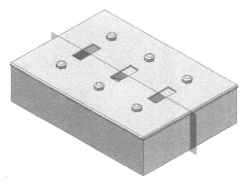

Figure 2–53

5. Save all files and close the window.

Practice 2d | iPart Member Tables

Practice Objectives

- Replace the iPart factory instance that is displayed in a drawing view with another instance.
- Place an iPart member table in a drawing to display its factory members and their attributes.

In this practice, you practice switching a view of an iPart to an alternate member. In addition you will create a table of the iParts, as shown in Figure 2–54.

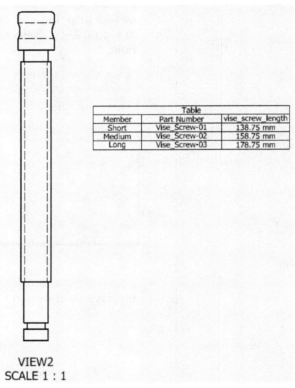

Table		
Member	Part Number	vise_screw_length
Short	Vise_Screw-01	138.75 mm
Medium	Vise_Screw-02	158.75 mm
Long	Vise_Screw-03	178.75 mm

VIEW2
SCALE 1 : 1

Figure 2–54

Task 1 - Switch the views to display an alternate iPart member.

1. Open **Vise_screw.dwg** from the *iPart Table* folder. The drawing displays as shown in Figure 2–55. The views reference **Short.ipt**, which is a member of Vise_Screw iPart. The three members of the iPart factory vary only in length.

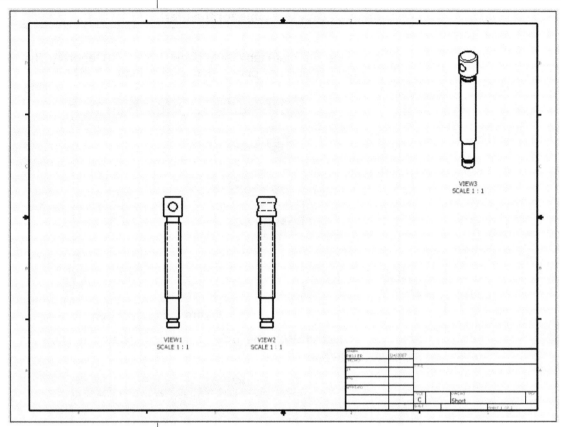

Figure 2–55

2. Right-click the isometric view (View 3, top right corner) and select **Edit View**. The Drawing View dialog box opens.

3. Select the *Model State* tab as shown in Figure 2–56. The *Member* area displays a list of the available iPart members you can display in the drawing views.

Figure 2–56

4. In the *Member* drop-down list, select **Long** and click **OK**. The views all update to display the newly selected iPart member.

5. Select the View labels and move them below their view.

Task 2 - Create a table for the iPart.

1. In the *Annotate* tab>Table panel, click  (General). The Table dialog box opens as shown in Figure 2–57.

Figure 2–57

2. Select **VIEW2**. The Table dialog box updates as shown in Figure 2–58.

Figure 2–58

3. Click (Column Chooser). The Table Column Chooser dialog box opens.

4. With Part Number selected in the *Available Columns* area, click **Add** to move the column property to the *Selected Columns* area.

5. Add the **vise_screw_length** property to the *Selected Columns* area as well. The Table Column Chooser displays as shown in Figure 2–59.

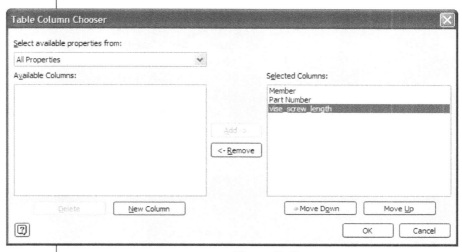

Figure 2–59

6. Click **OK** to close the Table Column Chooser dialog box.

7. Click **OK** to close the Table dialog box.

8. Move the cursor to the right of **VIEW2** and click to place it. The table populates with the columns and attributes of the iPart factory members and displays as shown in Figure 2–60.

Table		
Member	Part Number	vise_screw_length
Short	Vise_Screw-01	138.75 mm
Medium	Vise_Screw-02	158.75 mm
Long	Vise_Screw-03	178.75 mm

Figure 2–60

9. Save and close the drawing.

Chapter Review Questions

1. Which of the following best describes the difference between a standard iPart Factory and a custom iPart Factory?

   a. Custom iPart Factories include parameters that enables you to enter values when the iPart file is opened. In standard iPart Factories, all values for all parameters are preset.

   b. Custom iPart Factories include parameters that enables you to enter values when the iPart is placed in an assembly. In standard iPart Factories, all values for all parameters are preset.

   c. Both custom and standard iPart Factories include parameters that enables you to enter values when the iPart Factory file is used.

   d. None of the above.

2. Which of the following tabs in the iPart Author should be accessed to add features to the table so that they can be suppressed in iPart members?

   a. Parameters

   b. Properties

   c. Suppression

   d. iFeatures

   e. iMates

   f. Other

3. Which of the following can be entered in an iPart table to suppress a feature in a part? (Select all that apply.)

   a. Suppress

   b. Compute

   c. S

   d. C

   e. 0

   f. 1

   g. Off

   h. On

Refer to Figure 2–61 when answering Questions 4 and 5 below:

	💾	Member	Part Number	🔍 stub_len	🔍 major_dia	minor_dia	grip_len 🔍	Thread2: Designation
1		hex_bolt_ipart_final-01	hex_bolt_ipart_final-01	30 mm	4.974 mm	4.11 mm	2.4 mm	M5x0.8
2		hex_bolt_ipart_final-02	hex_bolt_ipart_final-02	30 mm	5.974 mm	4.891 mm	3 mm	M6x1
3		hex_bolt_ipart_final-03	hex_bolt_ipart_final-03	30 mm	9.968 mm	8.344 mm	4.5 mm	M10x1.5
4		hex_bolt_ipart_final-04	hex_bolt_ipart_final-04	30 mm	15.962 mm	13.797 mm	6 mm	M16x2
5		hex_bolt_ipart_final-05	hex_bolt-05	30 mm	4.142 mm	3.98 mm	3 mm	M5x0.8

Figure 2–61

4. How many Keys have been set in the iPart Factory shown in Figure 2–61?

   a. 1

   b. 3

   c. 7

   d. None

5. Which parameter in the iPart Factory shown in Figure 2–61 is custom?

   a. Part Number

   b. stub_len

   c. grip_len

   d. Thread2:Designation

   e. None

6. The equations that are entered in Excel cannot be changed in the iPart Author dialog box.

   a. True

   b. False

7. Which command should be used when adding a new feature that is only required in the active factory member?

   a. **Edit Member Scope**

   b. **Edit Factory Scope**

8. Which of the following drawing **Annotation** options can you use to document the members of an iPart factory in a drawing?

    a. Parts List

    b. Revision Table

    c. General Table

    d. Hole Table

Command Summary

Button	Command	Location
N/A	Change Component	• **Context menu**: In Model browser with Table selected
![icon]	Create iPart	• **Ribbon:** *Manage* tab>Author panel
N/A	Edit Factory Scope	• **Ribbon:** *Manage* tab>Author panel
N/A	Edit Member Scope	• **Ribbon:** *Manage* tab>Author panel
N/A	Edit Table	• **Context menu**: In Model browser with Table selected
N/A	Edit via Spreadsheet	• **Context menu**: In Model browser with Table selected
![icon]	Extract iFeature	• **Ribbon:** *Manage* tab>Author panel
![icon]	General (table)	• **Ribbon:** *Annotate* tab>Table panel
![icon]	Place (Component)	• **Ribbon:** *Assemble* tab>Component panel

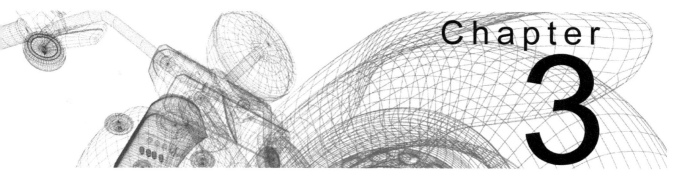

iMates

The iMate functionality in the Autodesk® Inventor® software is a design tool that enables you to work more efficiently with your part designs when assembling them into a top-level assembly. Using this functionality, you can define how the component will be constrained into an assembly and store this information directly with the component for quick and easy use.

Learning Objectives in this Chapter

- Build iMate constraints into parts or subassemblies to define how they connect with other components in an assembly.
- Combine multiple iMates into a Composite iMate group, so that multiple iMates can act as one.
- Convert constraints between components in an assembly to create multiple single iMates or a single Composite iMate.
- Manually or automatically match iMates of parts in an assembly.
- Control the order in which iMate pairs are previewed by using the Match List functionality.
- Vary constraint settings in iParts by including iMates.

3.1 iMates

iMates are constraints built into parts or subassemblies. They define how a component connects with other components in an assembly. You define iMates in a component by selecting a constraint type and its accompanying reference entity (e.g., face, edge, vertex, etc.) that is matched with other components. When you assemble components with iMates, you match the iMates from different components, manually or automatically. If you define iMates with the same names in two different components, the components become interchangeable in an assembly.

In Figure 3–1, the two mounting brackets have identical iMates defined, making them interchangeable in the assembly. You can replace one or the other without having to reapply the constraints.

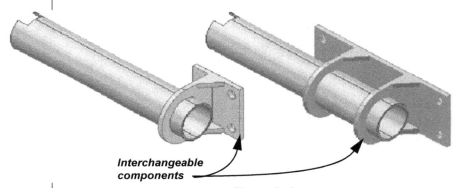

Interchangeable components

Figure 3–1

Creating iMates

To create an iMate, in the *Manage* tab>Author panel, click

(iMate). The Create iMate dialog box opens, as shown in Figure 3–2. Creating iMates is similar to placing constraints, except that you are only selecting the reference for one component. As with constraints, you select the reference (line, plane, point, etc.) on which you want to place the iMate, as well as set any offset or angle values. iMates can be created in part or assembly files. iMates added to an assembly are used when it is placed as a subassembly.

The 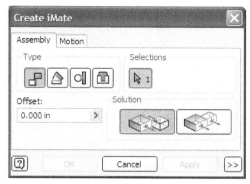 (Symmetry) constraint type is not available when creating an iMate.

Figure 3–2

Composite iMates

You can combine multiple iMates into a group, called a composite iMate. The composite acts as a single iMate and is applied all at once. Only one iMate symbol displays in the drawing window for each composite iMate. In the Model Browser, the composite iMate is listed above individual iMates in the tree structure.

To create a composite iMate, select several iMates in the Model Browser (hold <Ctrl> to select more than one iMate), right-click and select **Create Composite**, as shown in Figure 3–3.

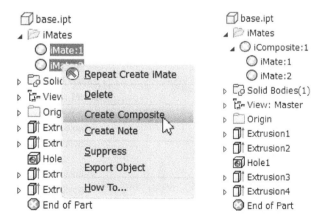

Figure 3–3

- To remove a single iMate from a composite, select the iMate in the Model Browser and select **Remove**. The iMate is moved outside the composite group.

- To delete an iMate or composite, right-click and select **Delete**. If you delete a composite group, all iMates contained in that composite are also deleted.

- To apply composite iMates at the same time, create a composite iMate with the same name in the other components you want to assemble to. When both components are added to the same assembly file, all constraints in the composite iMate are applied at once.

Creating iMates from Existing Constraints

You can convert constraints between components in an assembly to create multiple single iMates, or a single composite iMate.

How To: Convert Existing Assembly Constraints to iMates

1. Select the component in the Model Browser and select **Component>Infer iMates** in the shortcut menu. The Infer iMates dialog box opens as shown in Figure 3–4.

Figure 3–4

Alternatively you can right-click on a single constraint in a component to create an iMate.

2. Select **Selected Occurrence Only** to create the iMates based on the constraints assigned in the selected component. If you clear this option, iMates are created based on the constraints used in all occurrences of the selected component.
3. Select **Create Composite iMates** to create a single Composite iMate in the component. If this option is not selected, each iMate is created on its own.
4. Click **OK** to close the dialog box. iMates created in the assembly file are saved with the part files.

Using iMates in an Assembly

In an assembly, the iMates in parts can be matched manually or automatically.

How To: Manually Match iMates

1. Select the component to display the iMate symbol.
2. Hold <Alt> while you drag one iMate to its corresponding iMate on another part. The symbols for matching iMates become visible when you drag.
3. Drop the iMate once matched by releasing <Alt>.

How To: Preview iMate Pairs Before Placing a Component

1. Open the required assembly that contains components with previously assigned iMates.

2. In the *Assemble* tab>Component panel, click 🗗 (Place), select a component that contains iMates to assemble, and select an **iMate** option for placing them from the bottom of the Open dialog box.

    - 🚫 **(Interactively place with iMates):** Automatically matches iMates, enabling you to cycle through, accept, and continue to preview and accept any remaining available iMates.

    - **(Automatically generate iMates on place):** Places and finalizes component placement based on the first iMate match the system encounters.

3. Click **Open** to open the file. A preview of the first iMate match displays, similar to that shown in Figure 3–5.

    - The component is oriented to satisfy the constraint and the iMate constraint symbol indicates the constraint type and reference location on each component.
    - The Command Line in the bottom left corner of the Autodesk Inventor window indicates which components and iMates are in the preview.

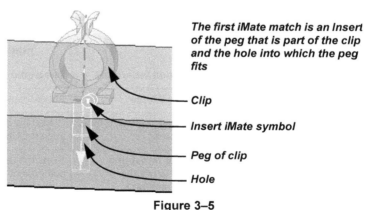

The first iMate match is an Insert of the peg that is part of the clip and the hole into which the peg fits

Clip

Insert iMate symbol

Peg of clip

Hole

Figure 3–5

When an iMate of a component is accepted and used to place a component, the iMate location in the assembly is no longer available to place other components.

4. When previewing pairs, you have the following options:

- Accept the iMate pair shown by left-clicking in the graphics window. If additional iMate pairings are possible and if  was selected, additional previews are shown. When a component instance is placed and no additional iMate pairings exist, you are returned to regular component placement.

- Press <Esc> to cancel component placement.

- Use one of the options in the shortcut menu, as shown in Figure 3–6. The specific options that are available depend on how many iMates exist in the component, as well as whether there is one or more matching iMate possibilities. The options are as follows:

Figure 3–6

Option (shortcut)	Description
Use iMates	Accesses and disables **iMate Placement** mode.
Place at all matching iMates	Places the component and all additional instances so that all iMate pairs are satisfied.
Skip remaining iMate results <Spacebar>	Skips the remaining iMate pairs and place the component with only the iMate pairs you accepted.

Generate remaining iMate results <Ctrl>+<Enter>	Accepts all current matches and any remaining are automatically accepted and used for placement.
Restart	Discards any accepted iMate pairs for the current component instance and begins previewing the iMate pairs again.
Next or Previous Component iMate (up and down arrow)	Cycles forward or backward between iMates. This option is grayed out if no additional iMates exist that are not already accepted.
Next or Previous Assembly iMate (right and left arrow)	Cycles forward or backward to another iMate of the assembly that matches. This is grayed out if no other iMates exist in the assembly that match the iMate in the component.
Next or Previous Instance Assembly iMate (<Ctrl> with the right and left arrows)	When a previously placed component in an assembly has been instantiated more than once and an iMate pair still exists for more than one of the instances, use these options to cycle forward or backward between the instantiations in the assembly. This option is grayed out if each component in the assembly is instantiated only once, or if the iMate in the other component instantiations has already been used.

Match List

The Match List functionality enables you to control the order in which the iMate pairs are previewed. This enables you to find the required iMate pairs more quickly, especially in larger assemblies or ones with many undesirable matching iMates.

How To: Add iMate Names to the Match List

1. Determine which iMates to match during component placement and rename them so that they have meaningful names to help distinguish them.
   - You can rename in the iMates folder in the Model Browser or by editing the iMate.
2. Open the component being placed in a separate window, in the Model Browser, right-click on **iMate**, and select **Edit**. The Edit iMate dialog box opens.

The Name and Match List areas of the dialog box are also available during the creation of an iMate.

3. Click 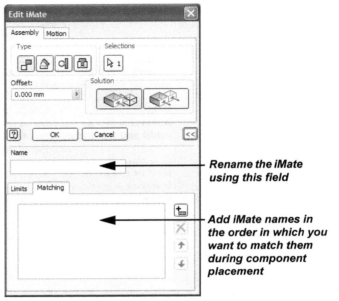 to expand the dialog box. Select the *Matching* tab. It displays similar to that shown in Figure 3–7.

Rename the iMate using this field

Add iMate names in the order in which you want to match them during component placement

Figure 3–7

4. Click [icon] and enter the name of the iMate to which you want to match the iMate you are editing and press <Enter>.

5. Add additional iMate names from either the same or any other components, as required.

6. Use [up] and [down] to move the iMate names up and down in the list as required.

- The higher up an iMate is in the Match List, the sooner it displays when iMate pairs are previewed.

A sample Match List is shown in Figure 3–8.

When a component is placed in an assembly, its iMates are matched with other components. The iMate first looks to the Match Lists and tries to match hole_parallel. If no match is found, clip-hole_parallel is reviewed. If a match is found a preview is displayed. If no match is found, matching would continue to the next iMate in the same or other components.

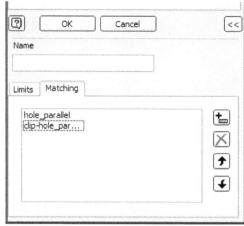

Figure 3–8

7. Click **OK** to complete the modification to the iMate.
8. Edit other iMates in the same component and add names to their Match Lists. Reorder the names as required.

Hint: iMate Order and Match Lists

To ensure a particular iMate of the component you are placing is previewed before another, drag and drop the iMate higher in the list, in addition to adding its iMate pairing to the top of the Match List. As long as a matching iMate exists in the assembly in which you are placing the component, that iMate is the first iMate pair that is previewed.

Notes on iMates

When using iMates:

* Before an iMate is matched, the iMate symbol is displayed when the part is selected. After it is consumed, it is no longer displayed.

- In the Model Browser, iMates for each component are listed in a folder beneath the component. After the iMates are applied, a separate symbol displays indicating the constraint, as shown in Figure 3–9.

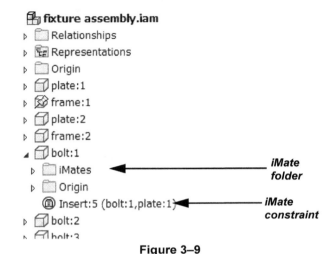

Figure 3–9

- The type of iMate determines the symbol. For example, the iMate symbol looks different from the Insert symbol, as shown in Figure 3–10. To display the symbol (glyphs), in the View tab>Visibility panel, click ⊗ (iMate Glyph).

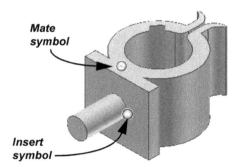

Figure 3–10

- Both iMates must be defined with the same offset, angle, rotation, or direction.

- You can use a combination of iMates and regular constraints to assemble components.

iMates in iParts

iMates can be included in iParts to vary constraint settings (e.g., offset or angle) in iPart instances. In the *Manage* tab>Author panel, click 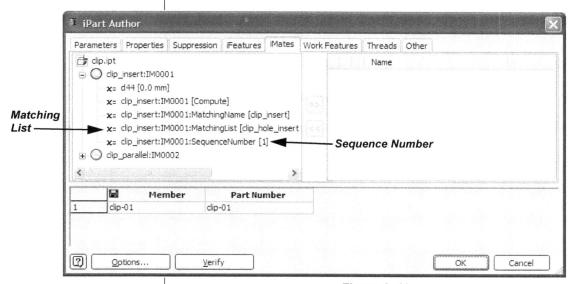 (Create iPart) to open the iPart Author dialog box and use the *iMates* tab, as shown in Figure 3–11.

Figure 3–11

The iMate can be suppressed in an iPart instance so that it is not present. **iMate** parameters can be used as keys in an iPart. You can also add the following information to the iPart factory:

- The iMate **Sequence Number** sets the order in which iMates are applied so that they are matched automatically.

- The iMate **Matching List** automatically matches to an iMate of the same name in the assembly.

Practice 3a | iMates

Practice Objectives

- Place components into an assembly using iMates and cycling through various methods, while observing some of the available options.
- Customize the order of the iMate pairing previews by using the Match List functionality.

In this practice, you will place components into an assembly using iMates. You will also use the Match List functionality to customize the order of the iMate pairing previews. The design intent is to assemble components more quickly and efficiently through the use of iMates. You will place bolts and clips into the fixture assembly shown in Figure 3–12, using the iMate placement mode.

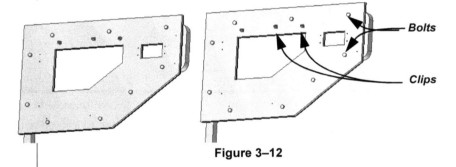

Figure 3–12

Task 1 - Open an assembly file.

1. Open **fixture assembly.iam** from the *iMates* folder. The assembly displays as shown in Figure 3–13. The fixture assembly contains two instances each of a frame and a plate. iMates have already been created for the plates.

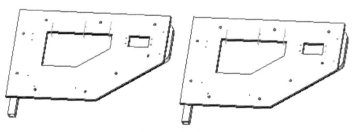

Figure 3–13

Task 2 - Preview and place instances of the bolt into the assembly.

1. In the *Assemble* tab>Component panel, click ![Place] (Place).

2. At the bottom of the Place Component dialog box, click

    ![icon] (Interactively place with iMates) to enable the use of iMates during placement.

3. Select **bolt.ipt** in the *iMates* folder, as shown in Figure 3–14.

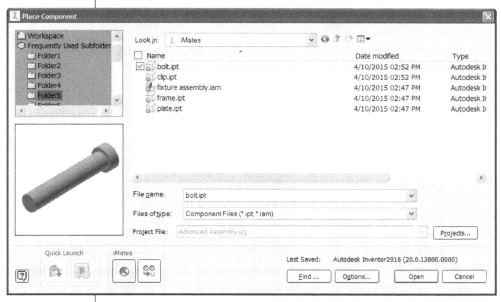

Figure 3–14

4. Click **Open**. A preview of the first iMate match displays, as shown in Figure 3–15.

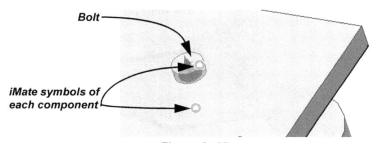

Figure 3–15

5. Click in the graphics window to accept the iMate. Because there are no other iMates, the bolt is placed in the assembly. A second instance of the bolt displays and a preview of the iMate pairing between the second instance and the assembly is displayed.

6. Right-click in the graphics window and the available options display, as shown in Figure 3–16.

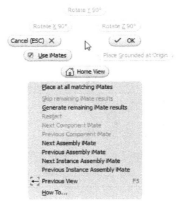

Figure 3–16

7. Toggle off the **Use iMates** option. The iMate placement functionality is terminated and the bolt can be placed as it normally would if there were no iMates.

8. Right-click in the graphics window and select **Use iMates** to switch back to the iMate Placement mode.

9. Zoom out so that you can see the entire assembly.

10. Right-click in the graphics window and select **Next Assembly iMate**. The iMate pairing preview moves to the next iMate that matches the iMate in the bolt, as shown in Figure 3–17.

The iMate preview moves to the next matching iMate in the assembly

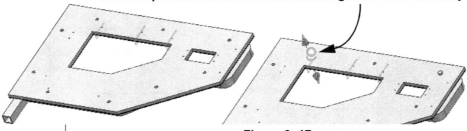

Figure 3–17

11. Move the bolt instance to the next assembly iMate.

12. Press <Right arrow>. The bolt instance moves to the next matching iMate in the assembly.

13. Press <Right arrow> several more times until the bolt instance moves to the hole shown in Figure 3–18, which resides in the plate on the left. None of the smaller holes on the plate were considered to be an appropriate iMate pairing with the bolt. This is because the iMate for the bolt was constrained with an offset of 1mm, which is the same offset that exists for each iMate in the larger holes. The iMate for the smaller holes, even though they are also Insert constraints that are in the same direction, have an offset of 0mm and are not recognized as an iMate pairing for the iMate in the bolt.

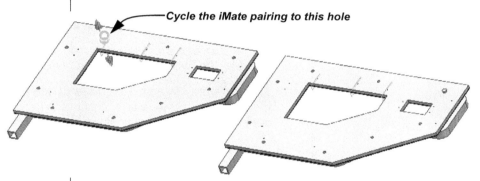

Cycle the iMate pairing to this hole

Figure 3–18

14. Use <Left arrow> to cycle the preview back to the hole, as shown in Figure 3–19.

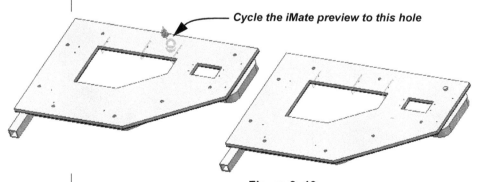

Cycle the iMate preview to this hole

Figure 3–19

15. Right-click in the graphics window and select **Next Instance Assembly iMate**. The iMate pair preview moves to the plate instance on the right side, as shown in Figure 3–20.

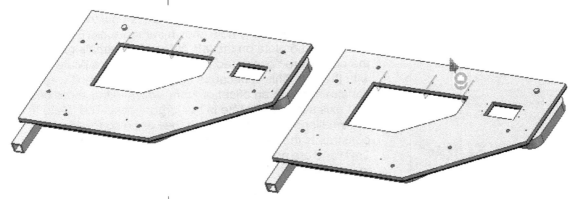

Figure 3–20

16. Hold <Ctrl> and press the right and left arrows to switch between the two instances of the plate.

17. There are only two different sizes of holes in the plate. Cycle the iMate pair preview to one of the larger sized holes, and click to accept the iMate pairing and place the component.

18. Right-click in the graphics window and select **Place at all matching iMates**. Instances are matched with all remaining and compatible iMates. You can use this option successfully because the other Insert iMates for the smaller holes are different. If the Insert iMates of both large and small holes were defined with the same offset and direction, a bolt would have been placed in all of the large and small holes.

19. Save the assembly.

Task 3 - Preview and place one instance of the clip into the assembly.

1. In the *Assemble* tab>Component panel, click ![icon] (Place). Ensure that ![icon] (Interactively place with iMates) is selected. Select **clip.ipt** and click **Open**. A preview of the iMate match displays, as shown in Figure 3–21.

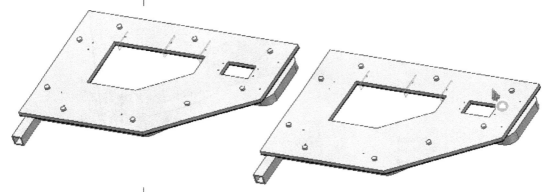

Figure 3–21

2. Cycle through the iMate pairing previews until you reach the one shown in Figure 3–22. You are required to cycle through many iMate pairings that you do not want before you get to the required hole.

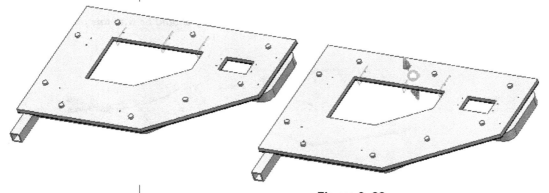

Figure 3–22

3. Click to accept the pairing of the Insert iMates. A second iMate exists for the clip. The type of constraint is indicated by the symbol shown in Figure 3–23. The names of the components and iMates that are currently being previewed are shown in the Command Line.

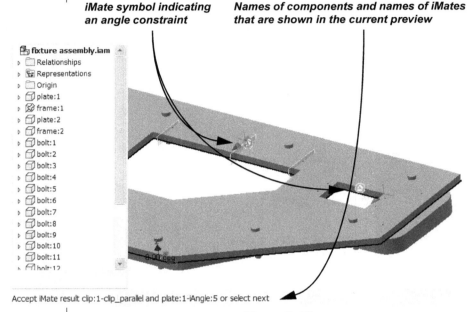

iMate symbol indicating an angle constraint   *Names of components and names of iMates that are shown in the current preview*

Accept iMate result clip:1-clip_parallel and plate:1-iAngle:5 or select next

Figure 3–23

4. Cycle through the iMate pairings until you reach the one shown in Figure 3–24.

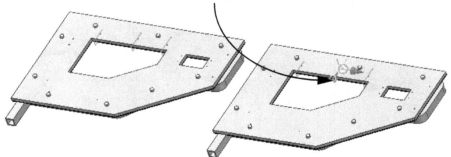

The iMate pairing should be with this plane

Figure 3–24

5. Click to accept the iMate pairing. The clip is placed in the assembly and a second instance of it displays.

6. Press <Esc> to cancel out of placing the component.

Task 4 - Edit the Match Lists of the iMates for the clip.

In this task, you edit the iMates for the clip so that during component placement, the initial iMate pairings are the ones required. This reduces the amount of cycling required and helps avoid confusion.

1. Open **clip.ipt** in a separate window. In the Model Browser, expand the *iMates* folder and note that two iMates already have descriptive names, as shown in Figure 3–25.

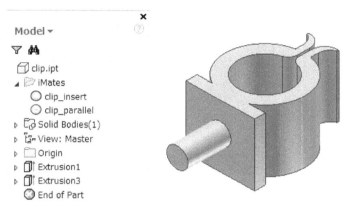

Figure 3–25

2. In the Model Browser, right-click on **clip_insert** and select **Edit**. The Edit iMate dialog box opens.

3. Click ⟩⟩ to expand the dialog box. A *Name* field is available where you can rename the iMate.

4. Select the *Matching* tab. A Match List specifies the order in which the system should look for matching iMates and preview them in the assembly. Currently, no iMate names are in the list. You are going to add one. First, you need to find out the name of the iMate to be added.

5. Cancel out of the dialog box and open **plate.ipt** in a separate window. The plate is the component that has the holes into which the clip is inserted.

6. If the iMate symbols are not visible on the part, in the *View* tab>Visibility panel, click 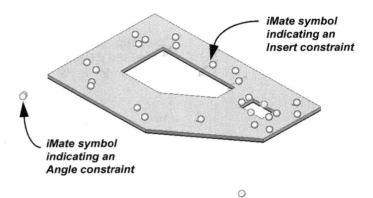 (iMate Glyph). Each symbol indicates an iMate that exists in the part. The plate displays, as shown in Figure 3–26.

iMate symbol indicating an Insert constraint

iMate symbol indicating an Angle constraint

Figure 3–26

7. In the Model Browser, expand the *iMates* folder and move the cursor over each of the iMates until you find the three Insert iMates that are shown in Figure 3–27. When you move the cursor over an iMate in the Model Browser, the corresponding iMate symbol in the model highlights. Note that the names of the three Insert iMates are **clip_hole_insert1**, **clip_hole_insert2**, and **clip_hole_insert3**.

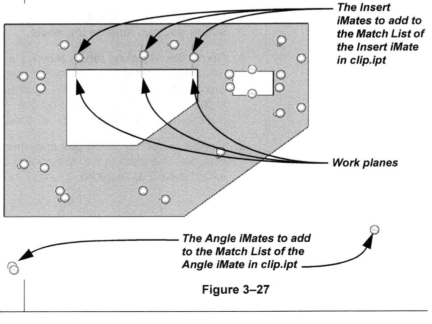

The Insert iMates to add to the Match List of the Insert iMate in clip.ipt

Work planes

The Angle iMates to add to the Match List of the Angle iMate in clip.ipt

Figure 3–27

8. Continue moving the cursor over the iMates in the Model Browser until you find the three Angle iMates shown in the Figure 3–27. Although the Angle iMate symbols display separate from the work planes (this is because the work planes were resized), the iMates do refer to the three work planes. Verify that the Angle iMate refers to a work plane by selecting it in the Model Browser. The corresponding work plane highlights. The names of the Angle iMates are **clip-hole_angle1**, **clip-hole_angle_mid**, and **clip-hole_angle3**.

9. Switch back to the **clip.ipt** window to add the iMates names in the plate to the Match Lists of the two iMates in the clip.

10. Right-click on **clip_insert** and select **Edit** to edit the iMate.

11. Click ⟩⟩ to expand the dialog box. Select the *Matching* tab.

12. Click 🔲 and type **clip_hole_insert2** as the iMate name to match with clip-insert. Press <Enter> when finished.

13. Add **clip_hole_insert3** to the Match List.

14. Add **clip_hole_insert1** to the Match List. Ensure that the underscores in the names are exactly as shown.

15. Select **clip_hole_insert1** and click ⬆ twice to move the name to the top of the list.

16. Click **OK** to complete the modification to the iMate.

   Any time a modification is made, that iMate is moved to the bottom of the iMate list. During the placement of a component, the first iMate in the Model Browser that contains a matching iMate in the assembly is the first iMate pair that is previewed. The specific iMate in the assembly that is first previewed is determined initially by the ranking in the Match List for that iMate.

17. Edit **clip_parallel**, expand the dialog box, and add the Angle iMate names from **plate.ipt** in the following order: **clip-hole_angle1**, **clip-hole_angle_mid**, **clip-hole_angle3**. Ensure that the names are exactly as shown and include the hyphen and underscore in the appropriate places to match the names of the iMates in **plate.ipt**.

18. Click **OK** to complete the modification to the iMate. **Clip_parallel** is moved to the bottom of the list of iMates. Because **clip_insert** is at the top of the iMates list in the Model Browser, it is the first iMate that is used for pairing during the placement of the clip in the assembly.

19. Save **clip.ipt**.

Task 5 - Place the clip into the assembly using the iMate placement mode.

In this task, you place the clip into the assembly using iMates. The first iMate pair preview is one of the required pairings. You will not need to cycle through before getting to the required iMate pairings.

1. Return to the fixture assembly. In the *Assemble* tab> Component panel, click (Place). Ensure that (Interactively place with iMates) is enabled, select **clip.ipt**, and click **Open**. A preview of the first iMate match displays, as shown in Figure 3–28. You did not need to cycle through any non-required iMate pairings before seeing a required one. This is because you added the Insert iMate names in the plate to the Match List of the Insert iMate in the clip.

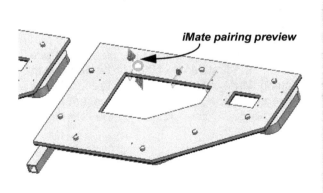

iMate pairing preview

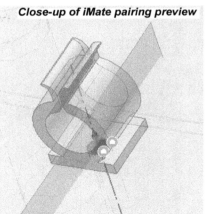

Close-up of iMate pairing preview

Figure 3–28

2. Click to accept the iMate pairing. The next iMate pairing preview displays, as shown in Figure 3–29. It proceeds directly to one of the iMate pairings that you do want. This is a direct result of adding the Angle iMate names from the plate to the Match List of the Angle iMate in the clip.

iMate pairing preview

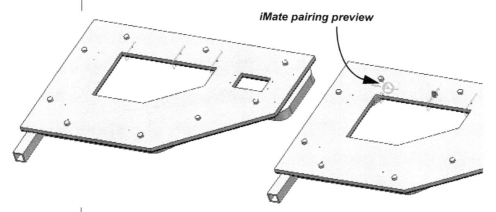

Figure 3–29

3. Click to accept the iMate pairing. The component is placed in the assembly using the two iMate pairings you accepted. Another instance of the clip displays and an iMate pairing preview is displayed, as shown in Figure 3–30. The next iMate pairing is with the same Insert iMate as the previous one, but on the plate on the left. The reason for this is because the iMate called **clip_hole_insert1** (which is in **plate.ipt**) is at the top of the Match List for the iMate called **clip_insert** (which is in **clip.ipt**).

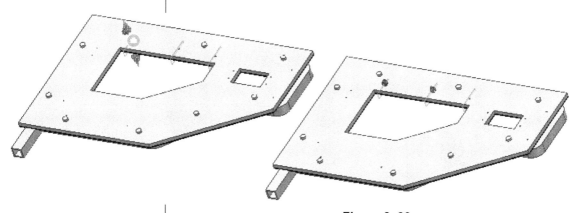

Figure 3–30

4. Continue accepting the previewed iMate pairings and placing the instances of **clip.ipt** until there are six instances in the locations shown in Figure 3–31. Recall that one of the instances was placed in an earlier task. Press <Esc> when finished placing the last instance.

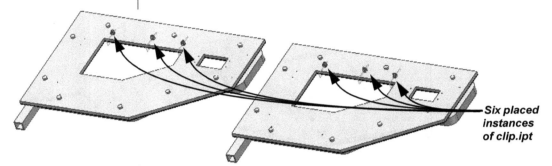

Six placed instances of clip.ipt

Figure 3–31

5. Save and close the models.

Practice 3b

Composite iMates

Practice Objectives

- Create multiple iMates and combine them into composite iMates.
- Assemble components in an assembly using iMates.

You will often place parts in an assembly using the same assembly constraints. iMates constraints can be defined in the part files, which tell parts how and where to connect when placed in an assembly. You can also combine multiple iMates into a group, called a composite iMate. The composite acts as a single iMate.

In this practice, you create iMates on three parts: you will group the iMates for each part into a composite iMate and then assemble them into a new assembly file. The three components of the assembly are shown in Figure 3–32.

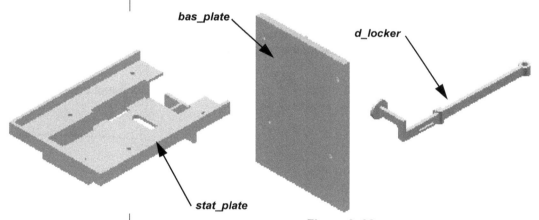

Figure 3–32

Task 1 - Open a part file and create iMates.

1. Open **d_locker.ipt** from the top level practice files folder. The model displays in Isometric view, as shown in Figure 3–33.

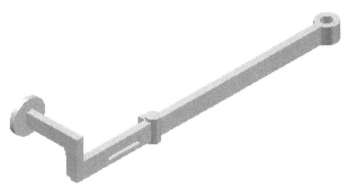

Figure 3–33

2. In the *Manage* tab>Author panel, click (iMate). The Create iMate dialog box opens. The Mate type constraint is selected by default.

3. Click to create an iInsert and select the edge shown in Figure 3–34.

Select this edge.
Note the orientation
of the part

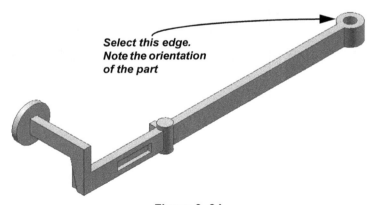

Figure 3–34

4. Click **Apply** to apply the constraint.

5. Click 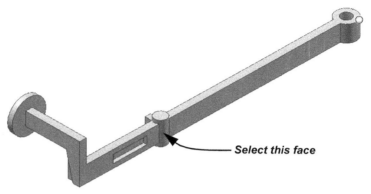. Select the outside surface of the feature shown in Figure 3–35 to create an iMate at the centerline of the round feature.

Select this face

Figure 3–35

6. Click **Apply** to apply the constraint.

7. Click **Cancel** to close the dialog box.

8. In the Model Browser, expand the *iMates* folder and select both the **iInsert:1** and i**Mate:1**. Right-click and select **Create Composite**. Then, expand **iComposite:1**, as shown in Figure 3–36.

Ensure that matching iMates have the same name in all models.

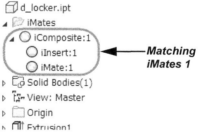

Matching iMates 1

Figure 3–36

9. Save and close the model.

Task 2 - Open the part called stat_plate and create iMates.

1. Open **stat_plate.ipt**.

2. Rotate the model, as shown in Figure 3–37.

3. Create an iInsert on the edge shown in Figure 3–37.

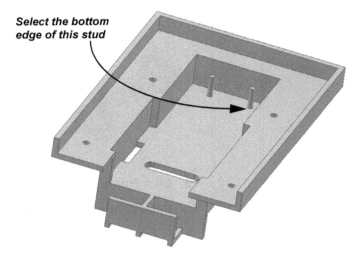

Select the bottom edge of this stud

Figure 3–37

4. Click **Apply** to apply the constraint.

5. Select the inside round surface of the slot shown in Figure 3–38 to create an **iMate** at the centerline of the round slot face.

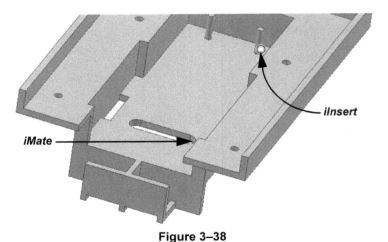

iInsert

iMate

Figure 3–38

6. Create an iComposite of the two constraints.

7. Create three more iMate constraints, as shown in Figure 3–39.

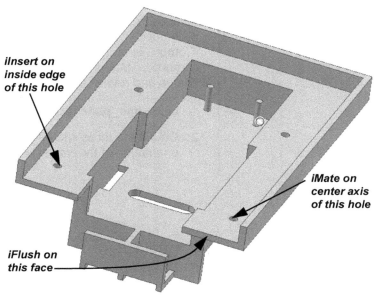

iInsert on inside edge of this hole

iMate on center axis of this hole

iFlush on this face

Figure 3–39

8. Create an iComposite of the three constraints. Expand the iComposites in the Model Browser, as shown in Figure 3–40.

Verify that matching iMates have the same name in all models.

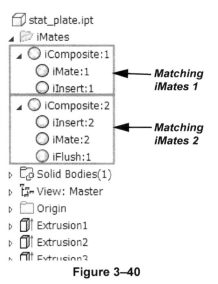

Figure 3–40

9. Save and close the model.

Task 3 - Open a part file and create iMates.

In this task, you create three iMates on the part, create a composite of the three iMates, and change the iMates and iComposite names to match the names of the iMates and iComposite in the previous task. This enables you to match composite iMates from different parts with the same number of iMates and names in an assembly.

1. Open **bas_plate.ipt**.

2. Create the three iMates shown in Figure 3–41. Note the orientation of the model.

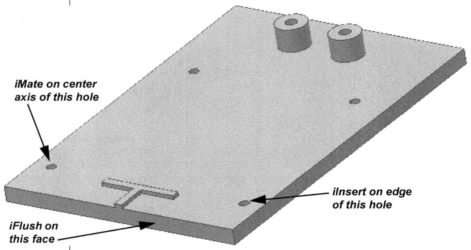

iMate on center axis of this hole

iInsert on edge of this hole

iFlush on this face

Figure 3–41

3. Change the *iInsert:1* and *iMate:1* names to **iInsert:2** and **iMate:2**, respectively. This ensures that the naming of the iMates match between components.

4. Create an iComposite of the three constraints and change its name to **iComposite:2**.

5. Save and close the model.

Task 4 - Create a new assembly file.

1. Create a new assembly file using the standard imperial template.

2. In the *Assemble* tab>Component panel, click 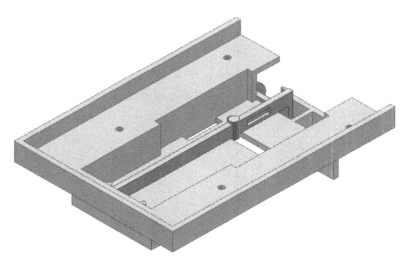 (Place). Ensure that [⊘] (Interactively place with iMates) is enabled, select **stat_plate.ipt**, and click **Open**.

3. Right-click and select **Place Grounded at Origin** to ground the component.

4. Press <Esc> to cancel placing additional components.

5. Click (Place) again. In the Open dialog box, select and open **d_locker.ipt**. The assembly displays, automatically assembled, as shown in Figure 3–42.

Figure 3–42

6. Click to accept the iMate pairing preview. The component is placed. Press <Esc>.

7. Place **bas_plate.ipt** in the assembly. The assembly displays, automatically assembled. Complete its placement, as shown in Figure 3–43.

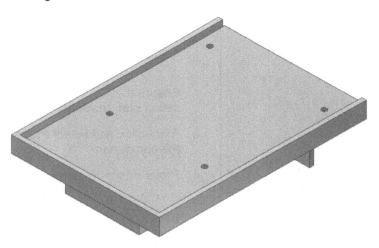

Figure 3–43

8. In the *Assemble* tab>Productivity panel, click (Degree of Freedom Analysis) and verify that there are no remaining degrees of freedom in the assembly.

9. Save and close the model.

Chapter Review Questions

1. Which of the following best describe iMates and constraints? (Select all that apply.)

   a. Symmetry can be assigned as an iMate but not as a constraint type.

   b. Offset and angular values can be specified when assigning both an iMate and constraint.

   c. Constraints can be incorporated into an iPart; however an iMates cannot.

   d. Constraints require references to be selected on two components while iMates require only one reference selection.

2. Once iMates have been used to locate a component in an assembly, it is not possible to add any additional constraints to further define its placement.

   a. True

   b. False

3. Which of the following best describe the purpose of a Composite iMate.

   a. A Composite iMate applies multiple constraints in multiple assemblies.

   b. A Composite iMate applies multiple iMates in one assembly, all at once.

   c. A Composite iMate groups all iMates of a a single type together.

   d. A Composite iMate applies multiple instances of a component at once.

4. Which of the following best describe the purpose of the Match List?

   a. A Match List create a list of similar iMates in an assembly.

   b. A Match List applies multiple constraints all in one step.

   c. A Match List controls the order in which iMate pairs are previewed and applied.

   d. A Match List adds iMates to iParts.

5. The iMate symbol associated with a component being placed in an assembly is displayed both prior to and after the component is placed.

   a. True

   b. False

Command Summary

Button	Command	Location
	Create iPart	• **Ribbon:** *Manage* tab>Author panel
	iMate	• **Ribbon:** *Manage* tab>Author panel
	iMate Glyph (display)	• **Ribbon:** *View* tab>Visibility panel
	Place	• **Ribbon:** *Assemble* tab>Component panel

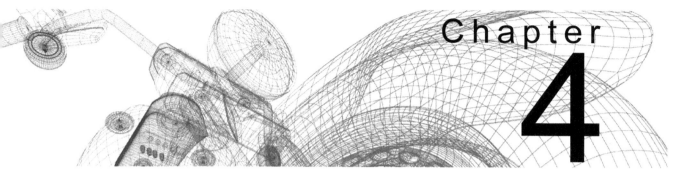

iAssemblies

Similar to iFeatures and iParts, iAssemblies enable you to quickly and easily create variations in your design. iAssemblies can help increase your efficiency by enabling you to create similar assemblies in a single file, instead of recreating them multiple times.

Learning Objectives in this Chapter

- Create an iAssembly that does not contain any components that are varied with their own iParts or iAssemblies.
- Create an iAssembly for an assembly that contains both iParts and iAssemblies.
- Convert components in an existing assembly to iParts or iAssemblies using the Replace option.
- Specify a member to use when placing an iAssembly.
- Edit the iAssembly Factory using the iAssembly Author dialog box or by using a spreadsheet.
- Define if components or features should be included in a factory table when added to an iAssembly.

4.1 Introduction

An iAssembly enables you to quickly and easily create variations in your design. Use them to create similar assemblies in a single file instead of recreating similar assemblies multiple times as separate files. To start, you set up configurable attributes that you can use to create the variations. These attributes can include the inclusion/exclusion of a component, use of members of an iAssembly or iPart, the offset value of a constraint, the material property, and the BOM structure of a component.

Examples of an iAssembly containing iParts and an iAssembly (as a subassembly) are shown in Figure 4–1. The three configurations (or members in the iAssembly factory) in the vise iAssembly vary in length and width. The table that contains all the iAssembly information is shown at the bottom of Figure 4–1. In this example, the only configurable items added are four iParts (**Sliding_Jaw:1**, **Jaw_Plate:1**, **Jaw_Plate:2**, and **Base:1**) and one iAssembly (**Screw_Sub_Assy**). The three configurations of the vise iAssembly vary by using different members of the four iPart and one iAssembly (the **Screw_Sub_Assy**).

In this iAssembly configuration called Large, the Base:1 part is an iPart that has been set to use the iPart configuration called Base_LargeWidth+LargeLength

Screw_Sub_Assy   *Base:1*

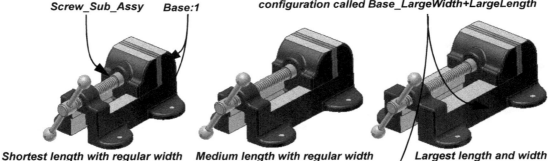

Shortest length with regular width   *Medium length with regular width*   *Largest length and width*

	Member	Part Number	Base:1: Table Replace	Sliding_Jaw:1: Table Replace	Screw_Sub:1: Table Replace	Jaw_Plate:1: Table Replace	Jaw_Plate:2: Table Replace
1	Vise_iAssembly-01	Vise-small-01	Base_SmallWidth+SmallLength	Sliding_Jaw-01	Screw_Sub-short	Jaw_Plate-01	Jaw_Plate-01
2	Vise_iAssembly-02	Vise-small-02	Base_SmallWidth+MedLength	Sliding_Jaw-01	Screw_Sub-medium	Jaw_Plate-01	Jaw_Plate-01
3	Vise_iAssembly-03	Vise-small-03	Base_LargeWidth+LargeLength	Sliding_Jaw-02	Screw_Sub-long	Jaw_Plate-02	Jaw_Plate-02

The vise iAssembly above is driven by this table

Figure 4–1

4.2 Create Basic iAssemblies

General Steps

If you have a part that varies and is within a subassembly, you must create an iAssembly for that subassembly.

Use the following general steps to create an iAssembly that requires no iAssembly subassemblies:

1. Create iParts for the parts in the assembly that are going to vary.
2. Create and assemble the parts into a new assembly.
3. Start the creation of the iAssembly.
4. Add configurable attributes.
5. Add iAssembly members.
6. Specify the required values for each iAssembly member.
7. Verify the iAssembly.
8. Complete the iAssembly.

Step 1 - Create iParts for the parts in the assembly that are going to vary.

Evaluate which parts in the assembly are going to vary and then create them, as required, using iParts. Some ways in which a part can vary and be handled by iParts include the following:

- The size of a dimension.

- The value of a parameter in the parameter list.

- The values of the properties in the *Summary* and *Project* tabs in the Properties dialog box.

- The suppression state (on or off) of a feature.

- The specifications of a thread.

- The offset value, suppression state, sequence number, matching name (in the match list), and name for an iMate.

Step 2 - Create and assemble the parts into a new assembly.

If you created a copy of the original part and converted it to an iPart, ensure that you assemble the iPart file rather than the original.

Once all required iParts have been created, create a new assembly. Assemble and constrain all the components in the new assembly.

Step 3 - Start the creation of the iAssembly.

In the *Manage* tab>Author panel, click 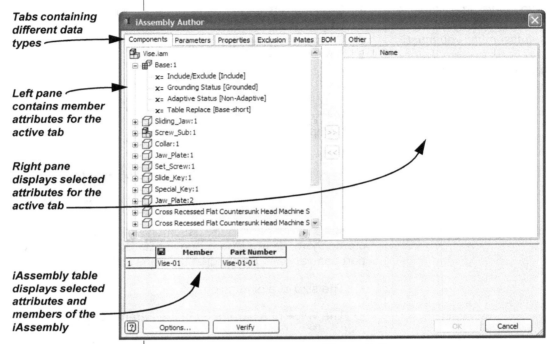 (Create iAssembly). The iAssembly Author opens, as shown in Figure 4–2.

Tabs containing different data types

Left pane contains member attributes for the active tab

Right pane displays selected attributes for the active tab

iAssembly table displays selected attributes and members of the iAssembly

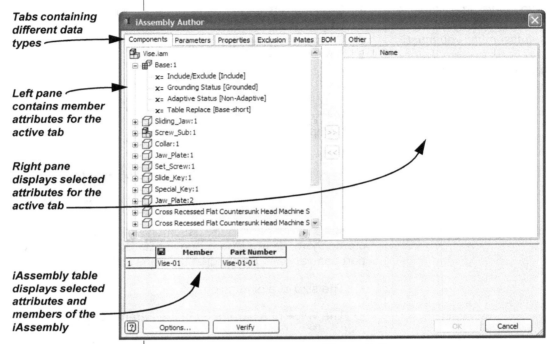

Figure 4–2

Step 4 - Add configurable attributes.

Keys can be defined in the same manner as they are for iParts.

To add a configurable attribute, select the tab that contains the attribute, expand the required branches to display the attribute, select it, and click [>>]. The attribute is copied to the right pane and added as a column in the table, as shown in Figure 4–3.

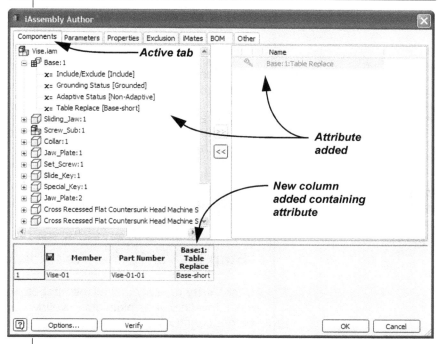

Figure 4–3

Add iParts to an iAssembly

The Table Replace attribute displays for iParts. Use this attribute to switch between the members of the iPart for different iAssembly configurations. Once added, a menu containing the iPart members displays when you select a cell in the *Table Replace* column.

Continue to add attributes from the various tabs, as required.

Step 5 - Add iAssembly members.

Right-click on a cell in the first column and select **Insert Row** (as shown in Figure 4–4) to insert a new iAssembly member.

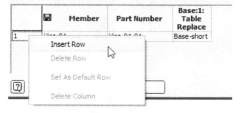

Figure 4–4

Step 6 - Specify the required values for each iAssembly member.

Select each cell and specify the required value for each attribute in the table.

If you want to customize the automatic naming of each part number or member name, click **Options**.

- Some cells require a manual input, while others provide menus of possible values. Change the member names and part numbers as required.

- Define the default member to use by right-clicking on the row and selecting **Set As Default Row**. The default row displays in green in the table.

Step 7 - Verify the iAssembly.

Click **Verify** to verify that all the attribute values you specified are valid. Invalid values highlight in yellow. Correct all invalid values before continuing.

Step 8 - Complete the iAssembly.

Once all required attributes and members have been added, click **OK** to create the iAssembly. By creating the iAssembly, the assembly is converted to an iAssembly. The Model Browser updates to show the members of the iAssembly, as shown in Figure 4–5. The checkmark next to an iAssembly member indicates the active member that is currently displayed in the graphics window.

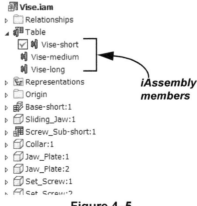

Figure 4–5

4.3 Create Multi-Level iAssemblies

If an iAssembly also contains subassemblies that have their own iAssemblies, consider the following:

- An iAssembly must be created for any subassembly that is going to vary, whether it is a direct attribute of the subassembly itself or one of its components. Follow the general steps outlined for creating a basic iAssembly. Save the file. Switch to the top-level assembly that contains the subassembly and update it. Redefine any constraints with undefined geometry (missing references). Create additional iAssemblies for other subassemblies as required.

- If a subassembly is an iAssembly, the top-level assembly must also be created as an iAssembly. Follow Steps 2 to 8 as outlined for creating a basic iAssembly. When assembling the components into the new assembly, ensure that you assemble the iParts and iAssemblies, rather than their counterparts that were not converted to iParts or iAssemblies (i.e., regular parts and assemblies).

Consider the vise assembly shown in Figure 4–6.

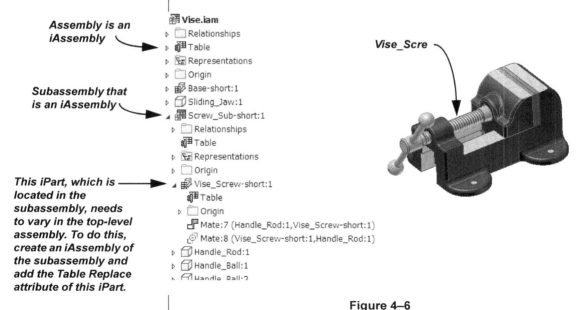

Assembly is an iAssembly

Subassembly that is an iAssembly

This iPart, which is located in the subassembly, needs to vary in the top-level assembly. To do this, create an iAssembly of the subassembly and add the Table Replace attribute of this iPart.

Vise_Scre

Vise.iam
▷ ☐ Relationships
▷ 🔳 Table
▷ 🔳 Representations
▷ ☐ Origin
▷ 📦 Base-short:1
▷ 🔲 Sliding_Jaw:1
▲ 🔳 Screw_Sub-short:1
   ▷ ☐ Relationships
   🔳 Table
   ▷ 🔳 Representations
   ▷ ☐ Origin
   ▲ 📦 Vise_Screw-short:1
      🔳 Table
      ▷ ☐ Origin
      🔲 Mate:7 (Handle_Rod:1,Vise_Screw-short:1)
      🔲 Mate:8 (Vise_Screw-short:1,Handle_Rod:1)
   ▷ 🔲 Handle_Rod:1
   ▷ 🔲 Handle_Ball:1
   ▷ 🔲 Handle_Ball:2

Figure 4–6

4.4 Create iAssemblies Using Existing Assemblies

Components that exist in an assembly and have been made into iParts or iAssemblies must be replaced in order to be recognized at the top-level assembly. In addition, the top-level assembly must be converted to an iAssembly.

General Steps

Use the following general steps to convert a normal assembly that does not contain any iParts or iAssemblies to an iAssembly:

1. Convert the parts into iParts.
2. Replace the normal parts with their iParts in the subassemblies.
3. Convert the subassemblies into iAssemblies.
4. Replace the parts with their iParts in the top-level assembly.
5. Convert the top-level assembly into an iAssembly.

Step 1 - Convert the parts into iParts.

You can keep a copy of the normal part before it is converted into an iPart.

Determine which parts are going to vary in the assembly. Open a part in a separate window, convert it into an iPart, and save the part. Convert the other parts that are going to vary in the same way, including subassemblies in the top-level assembly.

- After converting to an iPart, the Model Browser icon (🗄) for the component changes to include the image of a table, as shown in Figure 4–7. The component block is blue, indicating that the iPart factory is referenced. The component block is going to be yellow if an iPart member is referenced.

Icon before converting to an iPart

Icon after converting to an iPart. Note that the icon has the table being smaller in size in relation to the yellow block

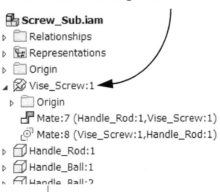
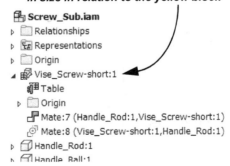

Figure 4–7

Step 2 - Replace the normal parts with their iParts in the subassemblies.

If you leave the factory referenced without replacing it with an iPart member, then the Table Replace attribute is not available for use in the iAssembly.

How To: Replace a Part

1. Ensure that the assembly in which the part was directly assembled is open.
2. Right-click on the part in the Model Browser, and select **Component>Replace**. The Open dialog box displays.
3. Select and open the iPart. The Place Standard iPart dialog box displays.
4. Select the member to replace with and click **OK**.

If any constraints exist that reference geometry on the component that was replaced, a dialog box opens (similar to that shown in Figure 4–8) indicating that a reference is missing. You must redefine the constraint(s) to resolve the issue.

If you are replacing multiple components, consider waiting to edit missing constraint references till all of the components are replaced. This ensures that additional failures are not created when other components are replaced.

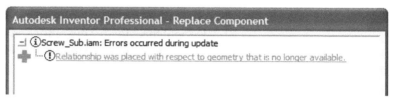

Figure 4–8

- After replacement, the icon changes to , where the component block is yellow. The name of the component also changes to that of the member designated upon replacement, as shown in Figure 4–9.

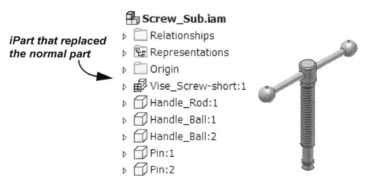

Figure 4–9

- By changing the component to a member of a factory, the Table Replace attribute is available for use during iAssembly creation.

Step 3 - Convert the subassemblies into iAssemblies.

You can keep a copy of the normal subassembly before it is converted into an iAssembly.

Determine which subassemblies are to vary in the assembly. If a part within a subassembly is to vary, then the part must be converted to an iPart before you convert the subassembly into an iAssembly.

- Subassemblies do not need to be replaced by their iAssemblies. However, when you switch to the top-level assembly, you need to update the assembly.

- Redefine constraints and resolve the missing references, if required.

- The subassembly icon in the Model Browser should change from 🔳 to 🔳 (the second icon has a red row and a red square) after the assembly updates.

Repeat this step for the other subassemblies that have attributes or contain components that need to vary in the top-level iAssembly.

Step 4 - Replace the parts with their iParts in the top-level assembly.

In the top-level assembly, replace the required parts with their iParts.

- If missing references are found, redefine them as required.

Step 5 - Convert the top-level assembly into an iAssembly.

Once all required components have been converted to iParts and iAssemblies, convert the top-level assembly into an iAssembly.

4.5 Place iAssemblies

To place an iAssembly, switch to the *Assemble* tab>Component panel and click 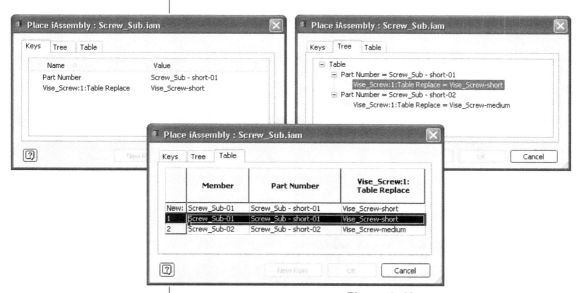 (Place). Browse to the file, and open it. The Place iAssembly dialog box opens, as shown in Figure 4–10. Use the dialog box to specify the member to use.

Figure 4–10

The three tabs in the dialog box provide alternatives for selecting an iAssembly member for assembly. They are described below:

- The *Keys* tab lists the values for each iAssembly member in the iAssembly Factory based on the keys that were created. Select the required value to make it current so that it is the member that is placed.

- The *Tree* tab lists the values for each iAssembly member in the iAssembly Factory in a tree structure. Expand the tree to see and select the required member to place in the assembly.

- The *Table* tab lists the values for each iAssembly member in the iAssembly Factory in a table. Select a row to make it the current member to be placed in the assembly.

Once you have selected the required iAssembly member, click a location in the graphics window to place it. After placement, the dialog box remains open to place another instance. Click **Dismiss** when no additional instances are required.

4.6 Edit iAssemblies

Once you create an iAssembly Factory (iAssembly file), you can edit it.

How To: Edit the iAssembly Factory

1. Open the iAssembly Factory as you would any assembly file.
2. Right-click on ⬛Table in the Model Browser and select **Edit Table**. The iAssembly Author dialog box opens.
3. Add or change the entries and then click **OK**.
4. Save the changes to the file.

- An iAssembly can also be edited in Microsoft® Excel®. In the Model Browser, right-click on ⬛Table and select **Edit via Spreadsheet**. In addition to simply editing cells, you can also use formulas and conditional statements. These statements are displayed in red in the iAssembly Author and can only be edited in Excel.

*The **Edit via Spreadsheet** option can also be accessed in the Assemble tab> iPart/iAssembly panel. By default, this panel is not displayed in the ribbon.*

Adding Components and Features to an iAssembly

*The **Edit Member Scope** and the **Edit Factory Scope** options exist on the Assemble tab (when displayed), and the Manage tab.*

When deciding to add a component to an assembly that is an iAssembly, considering the scope of the change is important. Consider whether the new component should display in only the active factory member or reflect in all factory members. The **Edit Member Scope** and **Edit Factory Scope** options enable you to control the scope of change.

- By default, the scope is automatically set to change the entire factory (**Edit Factory Scope**). If a component is added to an existing iAssembly, it is added to all members of the factory and no changes are made to the iAssembly table.

- If **Edit Member Scope** is specified and a component is added, it is automatically added to the table. The component's cell for the active member is marked *Include*. Other members are automatically marked *Exclude*, but can be modified if required.

The **Edit Member Scope** and the **Edit Factory Scope** options can be used in the same way to control the scope of features that are added at the assembly level.

Practice 4a | iAssembly

Practice Objective

- Create variations of an assembly without having to recreate similar assemblies multiple times by converting it into an iAssembly.

In this practice, you will convert the vise assembly into an iAssembly. The design intent is to create variations of the vise assembly without having to recreate similar assemblies multiple times. You want to be able to quickly open three specific lengths of the vise assembly, as shown in Figure 4–11.

Figure 4–11

Task 1 - Examine the vise assembly.

1. Open **Vise.iam** from the *iAssembly* folder. The assembly displays as shown in Figure 4–12. It is currently a normal assembly. You will convert it into an iAssembly.

🖳 **Vise.iam**
- ▷ ☐ Relationships
- ▷ 🔚 Representations
- ▷ ☐ Origin
- ▷ 🔯 Base:1
- ▷ 🗇 Sliding_Jaw:1
- ▷ 🖳 Screw_Sub:1
- ▷ 🗇 Collar:1
- ▷ 🗇 Jaw_Plate:1
- ▷ 🗇 Jaw_Plate:2
- ▷ 🗇 Set_Screw:1
- ▷ 🗇 Set_Screw:2
- ▷ 🗇 Slide_Key:1
- ▷ 🗇 Slide_Key:2
- ▷ 🗇 Special_Key:1
- ▷ 🗇 Cross Recessed Flat Countersunk Head Machine Screw - Type I - Inch 1/4-20 x 3/4:1
- ▷ 🗇 Cross Recessed Flat Countersunk Head Machine Screw - Type I - Inch 1/4-20 x 3/4:2
- ▷ 🗇 Cross Recessed Flat Countersunk Head Machine Screw - Type I - Inch 1/4-20 x 3/4:3
- ▷ 🗇 Cross Recessed Flat Countersunk Head Machine Screw - Type I - Inch 1/4-20 x 3/4:4

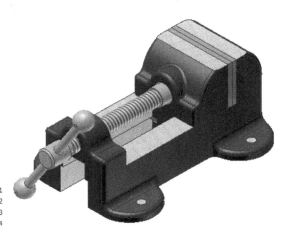

Figure 4–12

2. Examine the vise assembly to familiarize yourself with the model.

    •   Before creating an iAssembly, you want to understand how the model will need to vary to help you determine which components need to be converted into an iPart or iAssembly.

    •   Keep in mind the references that particular constraints are using. After replacement, you must redefine those references.

3. In the Model Browser, double-click on **Base:1** to activate the part.

4. Right-click on **Extrusion1** and select **Show Dimensions**. The dimensions of **Extrusion1** display.

5. Rotate the model similar to the position shown in Figure 4–13 to obtain a clear view of the 184.15 mm dimension. This dimension must vary, so the part must be converted to an iPart. Once complete, the iPart needs to replace the assembled component in the assembly.

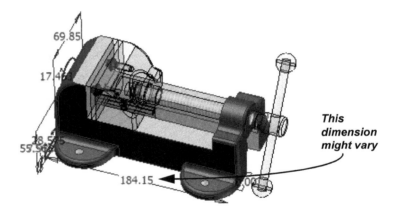

Figure 4–13

6. Double-click on **Vise.iam** to return to the top level assembly.

7. Expand the Base component in the Model Browser, if required, and select each constraint one by one. Note the references that are used for the constraints because they must be redefined after the iPart of Base replaces this component.

8. In the Model Browser, right-click on **Screw_Sub:1** and select **Open** to open the subassembly in a separate window, as shown on the left in Figure 4–14. The **Vise_Screw:1** part, shown on its own on the right, is the other component that needs to vary in length. Because this part needs to vary, it must also be converted to an iPart and replace the original component in the subassembly. Also, keep in mind that the **Screw-Sub** subassembly needs to be converted to an iAssembly because one of its components, **Vise_Screw**, will vary.

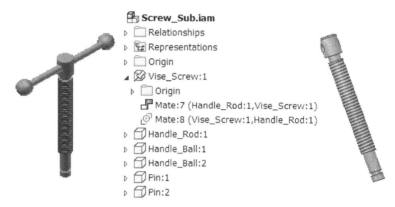

Figure 4–14

9. Select each Mate constraint in the Model Browser for **Vise_Screw:1** to understand how the part is constrained within the assembly. These two Mate constraints must be redefined after the component is replaced with its iPart.

10. Close all windows except **Vise.iam**.

Task 2 - Convert the Base part into an iPart.

In this task, you convert the Base part into an iPart because the component must vary in length.

1. In the Model Browser, right-click on **Base:1** and select **Open** to open the Base in a separate window.

2. In the *Manage* tab>Author panel, click ⓘ (Create iPart). The iPart Author dialog box opens, as shown in Figure 4–15. You should rename the parameters you use as attributes in your iParts for easy recognition. In addition, any renamed parameters are automatically added as attributes.

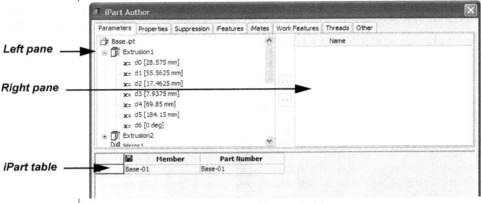

Figure 4–15

The other tabs contain additional attributes that you can add to an iPart.

3. Under **Extrusion1**, select **d5 [184.15 mm]** from the left pane and click ⟩⟩. The dimension is added to the right pane and to the iPart table, as shown in Figure 4–16.

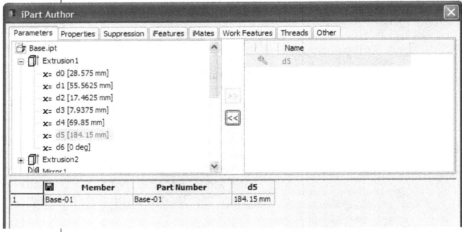

Figure 4–16

4. Right-click on the first row in the iPart table and select **Insert Row**, as shown in Figure 4–17. A new row is added into the table.

Figure 4–17

5. Right-click on the second row and insert another row into the table. The iPart table displays as shown in Figure 4–18. Three rows display in the table and each row is a member of the iPart Factory.

	Member	Part Number	d5
1	Base-01	Base-01	184.15 mm
2	Base-02	Base-02	184.15 mm
3	Base-03	Base-03	184.15 mm

Figure 4–18

6. Select the cell for member Base-01 in the *d5* column and type **164.15mm**. Press <Enter> to accept the change.

7. Change the cell for member Base-03 in the *d5* column to **204.15mm**.

8. Change the other cells to match the table shown in Figure 4–19. Click **OK** if prompted with *A Member name has been modified, which will alter the Filename of the member*. This message warns you that the file name of the member you are modifying has changed. The row highlighted in green is the default member that is used.

	Member	Part Number	d5
1	Base-short	Base-short	164.15mm
2	Base-medium	Base-medium	184.15 mm
3	Base-long	Base-long	204.15 mm

Figure 4–19

9. Select the row with the value 184.15 in the *d5* column, right-click, and select **Set As Default Row**.

10. Click **Verify** to ensure that all the cell values are valid. Any cells that contain invalid entries display in yellow. All the cells should be valid.

11. Click **OK** to finish creating the iPart. This iPart Factory contains three members called **Base-short**, **Base-medium**, and **Base-long**. The three members differ only in length.

Task 3 - Test the Base iPart.

Test the Base iPart you created to ensure that the different members behave as required.

1. In the Model Browser, expand **Table**. Double-click on the Base-short member. The part should display shorter.

2. Double-click on **Base-long**. The part should display even longer.

3. Switch back to Base-short.

Task 4 - Save the Base iPart and switch back to the assembly.

1. Save the Base iPart and close the window.

2. Activate the vise assembly window if it is not already active.

3. In the Quick Access Toolbar, click (Local Update) if it is available. Note the icon in the Model Browser next to **Base:1** now displays as . The component block in the background of the icon is larger than the table symbol that lies on top of it. This indicates that the iPart Factory is being referenced; however, none of the actual members are being used. To reference an iPart Factory member, you must use the **Replace** option to replace the Factory with one of its members. Recall that if an iPart Factory is used in an assembly, the Table Replace attribute is not available for use if the assembly is converted to an iAssembly. The replacement is performed in a later step.

4. Save the **Vise** assembly and accept to saving the Base part if prompted.

Task 5 - Convert the Vise_Screw part into an iPart.

In this task, you convert the **Vise_Screw** part into an iPart because the component must vary in length.

1. Open the **Vise_Screw** part, which is located in the **Screw_Sub** subassembly, in a separate window.

2. In the *Manage* tab>Author panel, click $\boxed{i}$ (Create iPart). The iPart Author dialog box opens and two attributes are automatically added to the right pane and iPart table. The two parameter attributes are automatically added because the parameters were renamed in the part. In this case, the **thread_length** parameter does not need to be included as an attribute in the iPart table.

3. Select the **thread_length** parameter attribute in the right pane and click $\boxed{<<}$ to remove the **thread_length** attribute.

4. Insert two more rows in the iPart table and change the values to display as shown in Figure 4–20. If the prompt *A Member name has been modified, which will alter the Filename of the member* displays, click **OK**. This iPart Factory contains three members called **Vise_Screw-short**, **Vise_Screw-medium**, and **Vise_Screw-long**. The three members differ only in length.

	💾	Member	Part Number	vise_screw_length
1		Vise_Screw-short	Vise_Screw-short	138.75 mm
2		Vise_Screw-medium	Vise_Screw-medium	158.75 mm
3		Vise_Screw-long	Vise_Screw-long	178.75 mm

Figure 4–20

5. Click **Verify** to ensure that cell values are valid.

6. Click **OK** to finish creating the iPart.

7. Test the **Vise_Screw** iPart to ensure that the length increases as you switch from the first member to the last member in the table.

8. Switch back to **Vise_Screw-short**.

9. Save and close the iPart.

10. Activate the **Vise.iam** window if it is not already active.

11. Update the model, if required. The icon next to **Vise_Screw:1** is 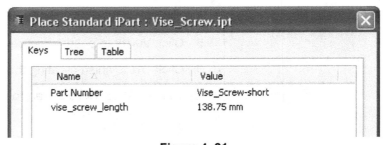, indicating that the iPart factory is referenced instead of an iPart member.

12. Save the Vise assembly and agree to saving **Screw_Sub.iam** and **Vise_Screw.ipt**, if prompted.

Task 6 - Replace the Vise_Screw Factory with one of its members.

In this task, you replace the **Vise_Screw:1** with a member of the **Vise_Screw** iPart Factory to be able to switch between the members of the Factory when you create an iAssembly for the subassembly.

1. Open the **Screw_Sub** subassembly in a separate window.

2. In the Model Browser, right-click on **Vise_Screw** and select **Component>Replace**. The Open dialog box opens.

3. Select **Vise_Screw.ipt** from the *iAssembly* subdirectory, and click **Open**. The Place Standard iPart dialog box opens, as shown in Figure 4–21. Use this dialog box to select which member from the iPart Factory you want to place. Each tab displays the same iPart Factory members and their attribute values in a different format. Therefore, only one tab needs to be used to select the required member. Use the tab that presents the iPart Factory member information in a way that you can easily select the required member.

Place Standard iPart : Vise_Screw.ipt	

| Keys | Tree | Table |

Name	Value
Part Number	Vise_Screw-short
vise_screw_length	138.75 mm

Figure 4–21

4. Leave the default member, **Vise_Screw-short**, with a vise-screw length of 138.75mm as the one to be placed and click **OK**. If a Server Busy dialog box opens, check to see if a Microsoft Excel window has opened. If so, switch to the Excel window and click **Cancel**. Close the Excel window and switch back to the Server Busy dialog box and select **Retry**.

5. The error dialog box opens, as shown in Figure 4–22. Click

   ✚ in the error dialog box. Click **Yes** to accept the changes and start recovering. The Design Doctor dialog box opens, indicating that Mate:8 has undefined geometry.

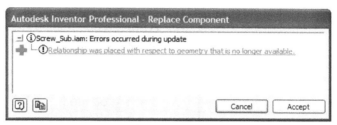

Figure 4–22

6. Select **Mate:8** and click **Next** twice to reach the treatment selection screen.

7. With **Edit** selected from the list of treatments, click **Finish**. The Edit Constraint dialog box opens. Only one reference is missing. The existing reference is an axis, highlighted in green on your screen, as shown in Figure 4–23.

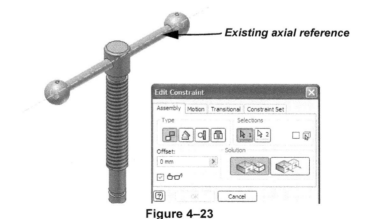

Figure 4–23

8. Select the axial reference shown in Figure 4–24 and click **OK** to apply the constraint.

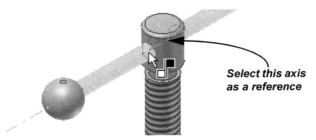

Select this axis as a reference

Figure 4–24

9. A new component now displays in place of **Vise_Screw:1**, as shown in Figure 4–25. The newly replaced component is a member of the **Vise_Screw** iPart Factory and the Model Browser displays the member's name. The icon next to it indicates that the component is a member of an iPart Factory that is grounded.

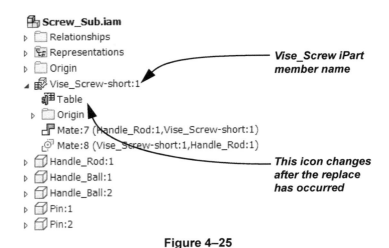

Vise_Screw iPart member name

This icon changes after the replace has occurred

Figure 4–25

10. Save the subassembly.

Task 7 - Convert the Screw_Sub subassembly into an iAssembly.

The **Screw_Sub** subassembly needs to be converted to an iAssembly because it contains a **Vise_Screw** iPart member, which you want to be able to vary in the top-level assembly.

1. In the **Screw_Sub.iam** window, in the *Manage* tab>Author panel, click 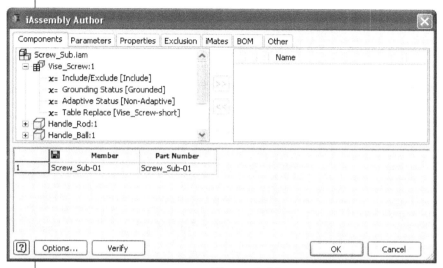 (Create iAssembly). The iAssembly Author dialog box opens as shown in Figure 4–26 and is similar to the iPart Author dialog box.

Figure 4–26

2. In the left pane under **Vise_Screw:1**, select **Table Replace [Vise_Screw-short]** and add it as an attribute. The attribute is added to the right pane and as a column in the table.

3. Insert two rows below the first row, as shown in Figure 4–27.

	🖫	Member	Part Number	Vise_Screw:1: Table Replace
1		Screw_Sub-01	Screw_Sub-01	Vise_Screw-short
2		Screw_Sub-02	Screw_Sub-02	Vise_Screw-short
3		Screw_Sub-03	Screw_Sub-03	Vise_Screw-short

Figure 4–27

4. For the **Screw_Sub-02** member, select the cell under the *Vise_Screw:1:Table Replace* column. Use the drop-down list and select **Vise_Screw-medium**.

5. For the **Screw_Sub-03** member, change the *Vise_Screw:1:Table Replace* attribute value to **Vise_Screw-long**.

6. Change the other cells to display as shown in Figure 4–28. If the prompt *A Member name has been modified, which will alter the Filename of the member* displays, click **OK**.

	🖫	Member	Part Number	Vise_Screw:1: Table Replace
1		Screw_Sub-short	Screw_Sub-short	Vise_Screw-short
2		Screw_Sub-medium	Screw_Sub-medium	Vise_Screw-medium
3		Screw_Sub-long	Screw_Sub-long	Vise_Screw-long

Figure 4–28

7. Verify the table values and click **OK**. The **Screw_Sub** subassembly has now been converted to an iAssembly.

8. In the Model Browser, expand **Table** and view the difference between the three members of the Screw-Sub iAssembly Factory by switching between them.

9. Switch back to the **Screw_Sub-short** member.

10. Save the subassembly.

11. Close the **Screw_Sub.iam** window.

Task 8 - Update the Vise assembly with the changes to the Screw_Sub subassembly.

---

1. Activate the **Vise.iam** window if it is not already active.

2. Update the Vise assembly. The error dialog box opens as shown in Figure 4–29.

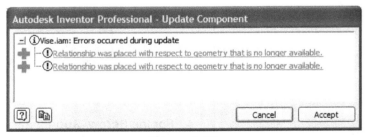

Figure 4–29

3. Click at the top in the Error dialog box and click **Yes** to accept the changes and fix the missing reference.

4. With **Insert:9** highlighted, click **Next** twice to reach the treatment selection screen.

5. With **Edit** selected from the list of treatments, click **Finish**. The Edit Constraint dialog box opens.

6. Select the axial reference shown in Figure 4–30.

Select this specific reference for the Insert constraint

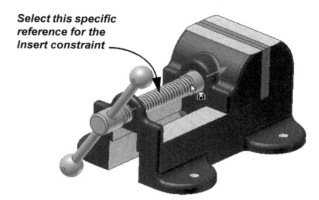

Figure 4–30

7. Click **OK**.

8. In the Place/Edit Constraint dialog box, click **Accept the relationship**.

9. Click ➕ in the Quick Access Toolbar to open the Design Doctor dialog box.

10. Click **Next** twice to reach the treatment selection screen.

11. Select the **Isolate and Edit** option from the list of treatments and click **Finish**. The Edit Constraint dialog box opens and only the **Screw_Sub** subassembly is visible because it was isolated.

12. Select the axial reference shown in Figure 4–31 and click **OK**.

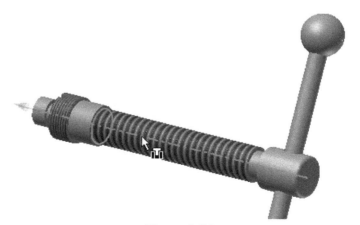

Figure 4–31

13. Right-click in the graphics window and select **Undo Isolate** to display all components in the assembly. If the other components still do not display, manually toggle on their visibility.

14. In the Model Browser, look at the icon next to the

Screw_Sub-short:1 subassembly. It now displays as ⊞. The colors of the symbol have changed, indicating that the component is a member of the **Screw_Sub** iAssembly and not the Factory.

15. Save the **Vise** assembly as well as the **Screw_Sub-short** and **Screw_Sub** subassemblies, if prompted.

Task 9 - Replace Base:1 with a member of the Base iPart Factory.

The last component that needs to be replaced is **Base:1**.

1. With the Vise assembly window active, in the Model Browser, right-click on **Base:1** and select **Component>Replace**.

2. In the Open dialog box, select **Base.ipt** and click **Open**. The Place Standard iPart dialog box opens.

3. In the *Keys* tab, select **164.15 mm** to expand the list of available values, as shown in Figure 4–32.

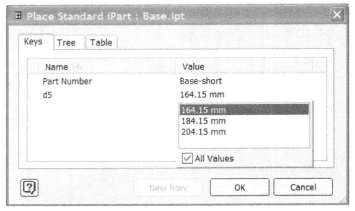

Figure 4–32

4. Select **164.15 mm** from the list to leave it as the member to place.

5. Click **OK** to complete the replacement. The error dialog box opens.

6. Expand the error. Click ✚ at the top in the Error dialog box and click **Yes** to accept the changes and start the **Recover** option.

In the next steps you will fix the missing references using the **Isolate and Edit** treatment option to redefine each constraint that contains undefined geometry. The references you need to select are shown in the following steps.

7. Select **Mate:4** and click **Next** twice to reach the treatment selection screen. Select the **Isolate and Edit** treatment option and click **Finish**.

8. For the **Mate:4** constraint, select the reference shown in Figure 4–33 and click **OK**.

Select this surface as the reference for Mate:4

Figure 4–33

9. Click **Accept the relationship** in the Place/Edit Constraint dialog box.

10. To make all components visible before continuing to redefine the next constrain, right-click on the graphics window, and select **Undo Isolate**.

Alternatively, you could leave the visibility of the other components toggled off since the only references you need to select are on the Base-short component.

11. Click ➕ in the Quick Access Toolbar to open the Design Doctor dialog box. Select **Mate:2** and click **Next** twice to reach the treatment selection screen. Select the **Isolate and Edit** treatment option and click **Finish**.

12. For the **Mate:2** constraint, select the reference shown in Figure 4–34 and click **OK** to complete the constraint.

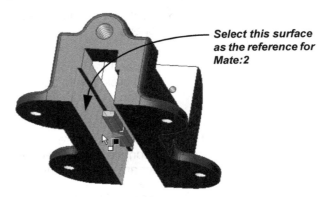

Select this surface as the reference for Mate:2

Figure 4–34

13. Click **Accept the relationship** in the Place/Edit Constraint dialog box.

14. To make all components visible again before continuing to redefine the next constraint, right-click on the graphics window, and select **Undo Isolate**.

15. As an alternative, in the Model Browser, expand the **Base-short:1** node, right-click on **Insert:2**, and select **Recover** to access the Design Doctor. Progress to the treatment selection screen. Select the **Isolate and Edit** treatment option and click **Finish**.

16. Select the reference shown in Figure 4–35 and click **OK** to complete the constraint.

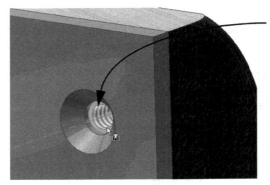

Select this reference for Insert:2

Figure 4–35

17. In the Place/Edit Constraint dialog box, click **Accept the relationship**.

18. Because **Jaw_Plate:2** is used as a reference for both the **Insert:2** and **Insert:1** constraints, you do not need to use the **Undo Isolate** option. You can continue directly into the **Recover** option to edit the **Insert:1** constraint. This time, you can select **Edit** instead of **Isolate and Edit** from the list of treatments.

19. Select the reference shown in Figure 4–36 and click **OK** to complete the constraint.

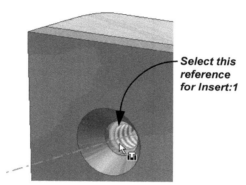

Select this reference for Insert:1

Figure 4–36

20. In the Place/Edit Constraint dialog box, click **Accept the relationship**.

21. In the Model Browser, right-click on **Flush:2** and recover the missing reference.

22. Select the reference shown in Figure 4–37 and click **OK** to complete the constraint.

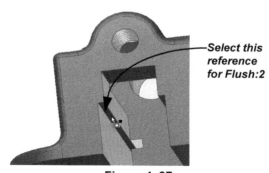

Select this reference for Flush:2

Figure 4–37

23. In the Place/Edit Constraint dialog box, click **Accept the relationship**.

24. In the Model Browser, right-click on **Flush:1** and recover the missing reference.

25. Select the reference shown in Figure 4–38 and click **OK** to complete the constraint. The errors should no longer display because all the constraints with undefined geometry have been redefined.

Select this reference for Flush:1

Figure 4–38

26. Use the **Undo Isolate** option to toggle on the visibility of all components.

27. Save the Vise assembly.

Task 10 - Convert the Vise assembly into an iAssembly.

1. With the Vise assembly window active, in the *Manage* tab> Author panel, click ![i] (Create iAssembly).

2. Select the **Table Replace [Base-short]** attribute under **Base:1** and click ![>>] add it to the table.

3. Expand **Screw_Sub:1** in the left pane, select the **Table Replace [Screw_Sub-short]** attribute, and click ![>>] to add it to the table.

4. Right-click on the *Vise-01* row and select **Insert Row** to add a row to the table. Repeat to insert a third row to the table.

5. Modify the iAssembly table to display as shown in Figure 4–39. Click **OK** if prompted with *A Member name has been modified, which will alter the Filename of the member.*

	🖫	Member	Part Number	Base:1: Table Replace	Screw_Sub:1: Table Replace
1		Vise-short	Vise-short	Base-short	Screw_Sub-short
2		Vise-medium	Vise-medium	Base-medium	Screw_Sub-medium
3		Vise-long	Vise-long	Base-long	Screw_Sub-long

Figure 4–39

6. Verify the iAssembly table values and click **OK** to complete the iAssembly definition.

7. Switch to each iAssembly member to view the change in the assembly. The length of both the **Vise_Screw** and **Base** should change.

8. Save the Vise assembly.

Chapter Review Questions

1. If you have a part within a subassembly that is going to vary, what would you need to do before creating an iAssembly of the top-level assembly? (Select all that apply.)

   a. Convert the part to an iPart.

   b. Add iMates to the part.

   c. Add iFeature to the part.

   d. Convert the subassembly to an iAssembly.

   e. Add iMates to the assembly.

2. Which of the following occurs when a subassembly is replaced with an iAssembly version of the same component? (Select all that apply.)

   a. Constraint references are lost and must be reassigned.

   b. The Model Browser icon for the component updates to reflect that it is an iAssembly.

   c. An iAssembly is automatically created in the top-level assembly.

   d. The iAssembly is marked as adaptive.

3. What causes cells in the iAssembly Author dialog box to be red?

   a. Invalid text entries

   b. Missing part

   c. Formulas

   d. Failed constraints

4. In the iAssembly Author dialog box, clicking **Verify** might result in the cells displaying in yellow. What does the yellow color indicate?

   a. Invalid text entries

   b. Missing part

   c. Formulas

   d. Failed constraints

5. When placing an iAssembly into a top-level assembly, which tab should be selected to view the iAssembly instances in the cell format similar to how the iAssembly was created?

   a. *Key* tab

   b. *Tree* tab

   c. *Table* tab

6. Which option adds a new component to only that instance of an iAssembly?

   a. **Edit Factory Scope**

   b. **Edit Member Scope**

Command Summary

Button	Command	Location
	Create iAssembly/iPart	• **Ribbon:** *Manage* tab>Author panel
	Edit Factory Scope	• **Ribbon:** *Assemble* tab> iPart/iAssembly panel • **Ribbon:** *Manage* tab> Author panel
	Edit Member Scope	• **Ribbon:** *Assemble* tab> iPart/iAssembly panel • **Ribbon:** *Manage* tab> Author panel
	Local Update	• **Quick Access Toolbar**
	Place	• **Ribbon:** *Assemble* tab>Component panel

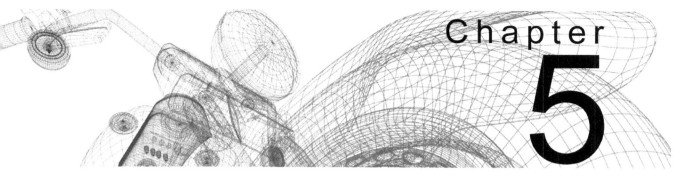

Chapter 5

Positional Representations

With Positional Representations, the Autodesk® Inventor® software enables you to create positional configurations of an assembly. These configurations can be used to review motion, evaluate the position of assembly components, or document an assembly in a drawing.

Learning Objectives in this Chapter

- Create and edit different positional representations of an assembly by overriding the existing settings of an assembly.
- Specify which positional representation is initially activated when the assembly is opened or inserted into another assembly.
- Find and edit Positional Representations more easily by viewing detailed information of only the Positional Representations that exist in an active assembly.
- Place Drawing Views of different positions of an assembly by using positional representations.

5.1 Introduction to Positional Representations

Positional Representations enable you to create positional configurations of an assembly. The configurations can be used to review motion, evaluate the position of assembly components, or document an assembly in a drawing.

Positional Representations are stored in the top-level assembly and can be retrieved or modified quickly and easily. They are listed in the *Position* folder under Representations only after the first Positional Representation is created. When the first one is created, a Master is also created. The Master Positional Representation is the default positional state of the assembly. The Master (default) Positional Representation of the excavator assembly is shown in Figure 5–1.

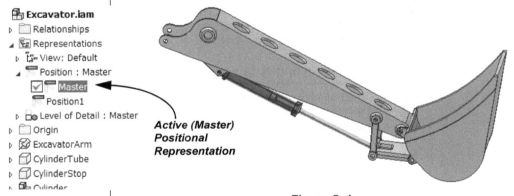

Active (Master) Positional Representation

Figure 5–1

When the Master Positional Representation is active, you cannot perform any of the modeling operations you normally do in an assembly (such as placing components, creating constraints, and saving the assembly).

5.2 Create and Edit Positional Representations

You can create new Positional Representations and make changes to the component positions and constraint settings without affecting the original component positions in the Master. An alternative Positional Representation of the same assembly is shown in Figure 5–2.

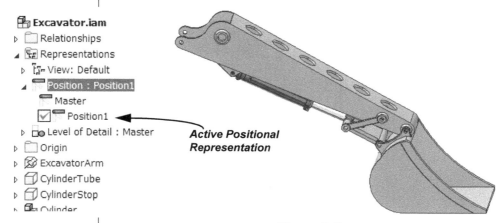

Figure 5–2

General Steps

Use the following general steps to create a Positional Representation:

1. Create a Positional Representation.
2. Override values for the Positional Representation.
3. Complete the override.
4. Modify overrides, as required.
5. Save the changes in the assembly.

Step 1 - Create a Positional Representation.

Expand the *Representations* folder in the Model Browser. Initially, no Positional Representations are available. To create a new Positional Representation, right-click on **Position** and select **New**, as shown in Figure 5–3. A new Positional Representation is created and activated, as shown in Figure 5–4.

| Figure 5–3 | Figure 5–4 |

- A checkmark indicates the active Positional Representation.

- You can rename it by clicking twice (not double-clicking) on its name and entering a new name.

Step 2 - Override values for the Positional Representation.

Verify that the required Positional Representation is active by double-clicking its name in the Model Browser or by right-clicking on its name and selecting **Activate**.

A Positional Representation is created using the Override dialog box to assign overrides to values in the Master assembly. Right-click on the object (such as a component or assembly constraint or joint connection) that you want to modify in the Model Browser and select **Override**. The Override Object dialog box opens, as shown in Figure 5–5.

Figure 5–5

*After modifying certain options and values, the software might move components to adhere to active constraints. If there are components you would like to remain fixed or grounded, set the Grounding override option to **Grounded**.*

Three tabs contain options that can be modified. Some options are grayed out, depending on the object type that you selected to override. All of the available options that can be modified are as follows:

Override Option	Description
Suppression (*Relationship* tab)	Overrides the suppression of a constraint or joint so that it can be applied in one Positional Representation and suppressed in another.
Value (*Relationship* tab)	Overrides a constraint or joint offset value to enable it to have a specific value in one Positional Representation and a different offset value in another.
Rectangular Pattern (*Pattern* tab)	Overrides the row or column offset value for a rectangular pattern.
Circular Pattern (*Pattern* tab)	Overrides the angle offset value for a circular pattern.
Grounding (*Component* tab)	Overrides the grounded status of a component.
Position Offset (*Component* tab)	Overrides the angle and offset positions of a component. The values can only be modified by directly moving the component in the graphics window. There is no value field in the Override Objects dialog box that can be directly edited.
Positional Representation (*Component* tab)	Overrides the current Positional Representation. This is valuable for setting a Positional Representation in a subassembly.
Flexible Status (*Component tab*)	Overrides the flexible status of a component. For a subassembly that is used multiple times in a larger assembly, you can make each subassembly instance flexible to enable each one to have a different position. For example, if the same hydraulic cylinder assembly is used twice in a larger assembly, one cylinder can be in a fully open position while the other is in a fully closed position.

For any option you want to override, enable the option by selecting it in the appropriate tab and setting the required values.

Step 3 - Complete the override.

Click **Apply** to apply the changes and continue to add overrides. Click **OK** to close the dialog box. The objects that have overrides applied display in bold text in the Model Browser and the override value displays in bold and in parentheses.

Step 4 - Modify overrides, as required.

The following options can be used to modify Positional Representations.

Copy

By default, a copy of the master representation is created when a new Positional Representation is created. In some cases, it is faster to copy an existing Positional Representation rather than the master. To do this, right-click on the Positional Representation to be copied and select **Copy**. A new Positional Representation is created with the same override values as the one it was copied from.

Delete

To delete a Positional Representation, you can either select the one to be deleted and press <Delete> or right-click on it and select **Delete**.

Edit Overrides

To edit an existing Positional Representation, ensure it is activated, right-click on the override (bold and parentheses), and select **Override**. The Override Object dialog box opens as it was when originally created and you can change the options.

To simply change a value associated with an override, right-click on the override and select **Modify (Override)** or double-click on the override (bold and parentheses) and enter a new value in the dialog box that opens.

Remove Overrides

An override for an object can be removed at once by right-clicking on the override (bold and parentheses) and selecting **Remove Override**.

Suppress Overrides

An override can be suppressed so that it is temporarily not incorporated into the active Positional Representation. To suppress, right-click on the override and select **Suppress (Override)**.

Step 5 - Save the changes in the assembly.

You cannot save an assembly while a Positional Representation is active. You must activate the Master in the top-level assembly and save the assembly. If you attempt to save the assembly while a Positional Representation is active, you are prompted to save the Master assembly. If you confirm the save, the model is automatically returned to the Master Positional Representation and is saved.

5.3 Use Positional Representations

Opening Files

If an assembly contains Positional Representations, you can specify which one is initially activated when the assembly is opened or when it is inserted into another assembly.

How To: Specify which Positional Representation should be Activated upon Opening or Placing an Assembly

1. In the Quick Access Toolbar, click 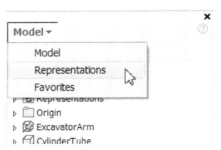.
2. Select the assembly to open or place from the Open dialog box.
3. Click **Options**.
4. Select the required Positional Representation to be activated from the Positional Representation drop-down list.
5. Click **OK** and then **Open**. The selected Positional Representation is loaded and activated.

Representations Browser

The Model Browser can be expanded to provide detailed information of only the Positional Representations that exist in the active assembly. This enables you to find and edit Positional Representations more easily. To enable expanded information for Positional Representations, select **Representations** from the Model Browser drop-down list, as shown in Figure 5–6.

Figure 5–6

Once enabled, all Positional Representations include the details on their overrides, as shown in Figure 5–7. Components and constraints that have not been modified are not shown in the Representations browser.

When in the Model Browser, right-click on an Override and select **Find Override** *to display the override in the Representation browser.*

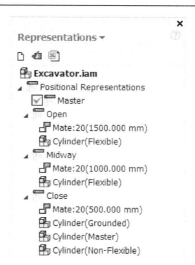

Figure 5–7

The icons available in the Representations browser are as follows:

Icons	Description
	Creates a new Positional Representation by copying the Master.
	Verifies all Positional Representations are valid and do not cause errors.
(only available if a Pos Rep already exists in the model)	Opens a Microsoft® Excel® table to edit the Positional Representations. Only overridden element values are displayed. Blank cells share the same value as the Master. Rows can be added to create new Positional Representations; however, you cannot remove, reorder, or rename rows. You cannot add new columns, edit column headers, delete columns or rows, or reorder columns.

Worksheet in Vise_POS_REP.iam [Compatibility Mode]

	A	B Mate:7 (Constraint Offset)	C Screw_Sub:1 (Positional Rep)	D Mate:7 (Constraint Suppress)	E Screw_Sub:1 (Flexible)
1					
2	Master	0.0 in	Master	Enable	Non-Flexible
3	Open	68.280 mm	Extend		
4	Free		Free	Suppress	Flexible
5					

Drawing Views using Positional Representations

To change the Positional Representation used in the drawing view, edit the view and select another Positional Representation. Any changes made to the Positional Representation in the assembly update in any drawing views in which it is used.

Positional Representations can be used in the Base and Overlay drawing views.

- To use an existing Positional Representation in a Base view, select the Positional Representation's name in the Position drop-down list, as shown in Figure 5–8.

Figure 5–8

- To document assembly motion in a drawing Positional Representations and Overlay views can be used together, as shown on the right in Figure 5–9. You must have at least two positional representations in the assembly to create overlay views. To create the view, select a parent view, define the overlay view options, and then click **OK**.

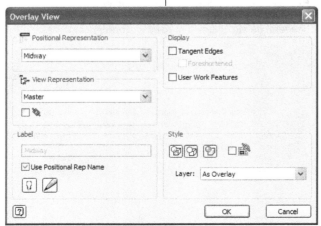

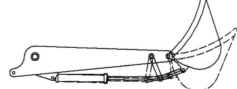

Overlay view is displaying both the Master view and a Midway view.

Figure 5–9

Practice 5a | Positional Representations I

Practice Objective

- Switch between different positions of an assembly by creating positional representations and overriding constraints.

In this practice, you create Positional Representations for an excavator assembly. The Positional Representations will enable you to quickly display three different positions of the assembly in the assembly or drawing environment. The positions are shown in Figure 5–10.

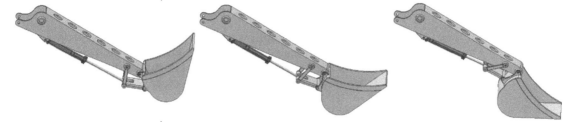

Figure 5–10

Task 1 - Create a Positional Representation.

1. Open **Excavator.iam** from the *ExcavatorAssembly* folder. The assembly displays as shown in Figure 5–11.

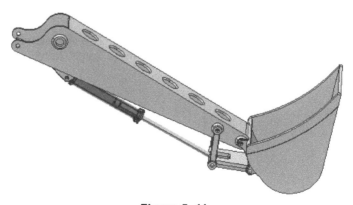

Figure 5–11

2. Expand the *Representations* folder, right-click on **Position**, and select **New**, as shown in Figure 5–12.

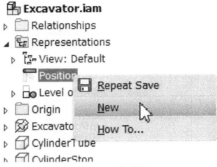

Figure 5–12

3. Expand the **Position** branch, there are two Positional Representations listed: the **Master** and **Position1**. A checkmark should display next to **Position1**, indicating that it is currently active and can be edited.

4. Rename *Position1* to **Open** by clicking twice on it in the Model Browser, typing the new name, and pressing <Enter>.

Task 2 - Create an override for the open position.

1. Expand the **Cylinder** subassembly, right-click on the **Mate:20** constraint and select **Override**. The Override Object dialog box opens.

2. Select the *Value* option and type **1500mm**.

3. Click **OK**. The model moves to the new position based on the new mate value, as shown in Figure 5–13.

Figure 5–13

Task 3 - Create an override to represent the mid-way position.

1. Right-click on **Position: Open** and select **New** to create a new Positional Representation.

2. Rename the new Positional Representation to **Midway**.

3. Expand the Cylinder subassembly, right-click on the **Mate:20** constraint and select **Override**.

4. Select the *Value* option and type **1000mm**. Click **OK**. The assembly now displays as shown in Figure 5–14.

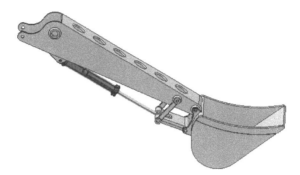

Figure 5–14

Task 4 - Switch between the three Positional Representations.

1. In the Model Browser, double-click on the **Open** Positional Representation. The model should update to the open position.

2. Double-click on the **Midway** Positional Representation. The assembly updates.

3. Double-click on the **Master** Positional Representation. The assembly updates.

4. Save the assembly and close the window.

*As an alternative, you can right-click on the Positional Representation and select **Activate**.*

Positional Representations can be used in the drawing environment to create Base and Overlay views.

Practice 5b | Positional Representations II

Practice Objectives

- Create Positional Representations with overrides to top-level and subassemblies.
- Display the Positional Representations of an assembly in a drawing.

In this practice, you create Positional Representations for a vise assembly to show its open and closed positions in a drawing. The two positions are defined by overrides in the top-level assembly as well as a subassembly. The drawing with an Overlay view showing the open position of the vise is shown in Figure 5–15.

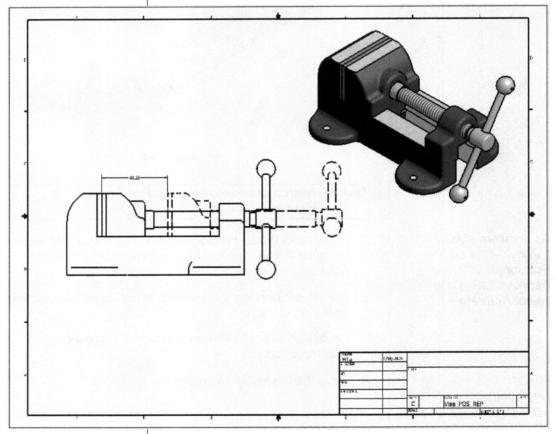

Figure 5–15

Task 1 - Open an assembly file.

1. Open **Vise_POS_REP.iam** from the *Vise_POS_REP Assembly* folder. The assembly displays as shown in Figure 5–16.

Figure 5–16

2. Review the Model Browser. The assembly contains one subassembly.

3. Open **Screw_Sub.iam**. Note that three Positional Representations are already specified in this assembly (Master, Extend, and Free).

4. Close the subassembly and activate **Vise_POS_REP.iam**.

Task 2 - Create an override for the open position.

1. In the Model Browser, expand the *Representations* folder, right-click on **Position**, and select **New**.

2. Expand the **Position** branch and rename *Position1* to **Open**.

3. Override the **Mate** constraint between the two jaw plates and specify a value of **2.7 in**.

4. Right-click on the **Screw_Sub** subassembly and select **Override**. By doing this, you can set a Positional Representation in a subassembly to vary in a top-level assembly.

5. In the *Component* tab, select the **Positional Representation** option and select **Extend** in the drop-down list, as shown in Figure 5–17. Click **OK**.

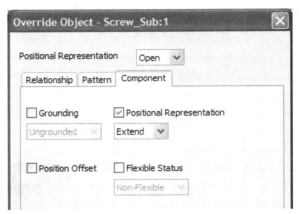

Figure 5–17

6. In the top-level assembly, create a new Positional Representation called **Free**. In this Positional Representation, you will suppress constraints and override a subassembly's Positional Representation so that you can drag components along their degree of freedom.

7. Override the **Mate** constraint between the two jaw plates, select the **Suppression** option and select **Suppress** in the drop-down list, as shown in Figure 5–18. Click **OK**.

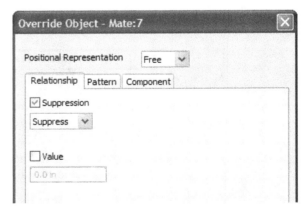

Figure 5–18

8. Right-click on the **Screw_Sub** subassembly and select
   Override. In the *Component* tab, override the Positional
   Representation for the **Screw_Sub** subassembly and set it to
   Free. Select the **Flexible Status** option and select **Flexible**
   in the drop-down list, as shown in Figure 5–19. Click **OK**.

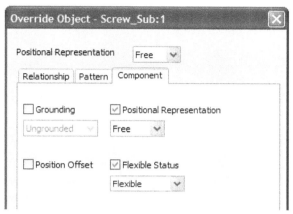

Figure 5–19

9. Select the **Sliding_Jaw** component and drag it in the
   assembly. Select the **Vise_Screw** (threaded screw)
   component and drag it back and forth. Note that these
   components are free to move when this Positional
   Representation is active. Otherwise, they are constrained.

10. Activate the **Master** Positional Representation.

11. Save the assembly.

12. Create a new drawing using the standard imperial drawing
    template.

13. Create a Base view of the assembly. Assign the **Left**
    orientation, the **Master** Positional Representation, and a
    scale of **0.75**.

14. In the Create panel, click 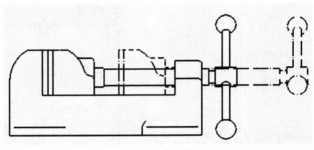 (Overlay) and select the previously created view as the parent view. Select the **Open Positional Representation**. Click **OK**. The view displays as shown in Figure 5–20.

Figure 5–20

15. To complete the drawing you can add a shaded, Isometric view in the right corner of the drawing.

16. Save the drawing using the default name and close all of the files.

Chapter Review Questions

1. How do you activate the Representations browser? (Select all that apply.)

   a. From the **Model Browser Representations** node.

   b. From the Application Menu.

   c. From the Model Browser.

   d. From the *View* tab in the ribbon.

   e. Right-click on an Override and select **Find Override**.

2. You can place new components in the assembly when you have a user-defined Positional Representation active.

   a. True

   b. False

3. How do you override values to create a Positional Representation?

   a. In an active Positional Representation, right-click on an object and select **Override**.

   b. In an active Positional Representation, modify the required values.

   c. Create a new assembly and modify the required values.

   d. Switch to the Override setting in the ribbon.

4. Which of the following statements are true regarding Positional Representations? (Select all that apply.)

   a. You can open an assembly so that a Positional Representation is automatically active in the model.

   b. When a Positional Representation is active, you must explicitly save the assembly.

   c. A copy of an existing Positional Representation enables you to start customizing its overrides based on the defaults in the Master.

   d. Subassemblies within a top-level assembly can have Positional Representations that are specified for display in a top-level assembly.

   e. Positional Representations can only be accessed and displayed in the assembly environment.

5. While working with Positional Representations, which of the following can you perform using an Excel spreadsheet? (Select all that apply.)

   a. Change values on previously overridden values.

   b. Create new Positional Representations.

   c. Delete a Positional Representation.

   d. Rename a Positional Representation.

6. Once a constraint's offset value has been overridden in a Positional Representation, the Positional Representation must be deleted in order to remove the override.

   a. True

   b. False

Answers: 1.(c,e), 2.b, 3.a, 4.(a,d), 5.(a,b), 6.b

Command Summary

Button	Command	Location
	Base	• **Ribbon:** *Place Views* tab>Create panel

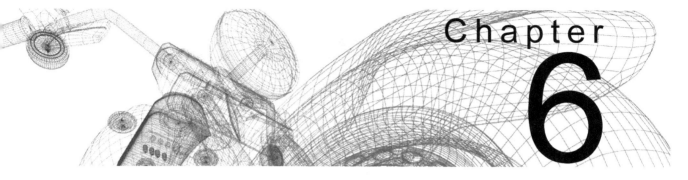

Chapter

6

Model Simplification

Model simplification is required by many designers as a method of large assembly management, incorporating place holder geometry into an assembly, or as a technique to simplify proprietary data going to an external vendor.

Learning Objectives in this Chapter

- Create a Shrinkwrap part that is a simplification of the original component.
- Selectively determine which assembly components to include in a simplified view and use that information to create a new part model.
- Define bounding box or cylindrical geometry to represent assembly components and use that information to create a new part model.
- Combine the use of a simplified view, envelopes, and visibility settings to create a new simplified model.

6.1 Shrinkwrap

The **Shrinkwrap** command can be used to aid in large assembly management. This command creates a derived part that is a simplification of the original component. The derived part can be a solid or surface component.

Some uses for the **Shrinkwrap** command include:

- **Large Assembly Management:** When working with large data sets, you can increase performance by removing unnecessary detail from the display. You can create a shrinkwrap part to act as a placeholder for entire subassemblies or for parts with many features.

- **Incoming Vendor Models:** In some cases, portions of a design might be modeled by a third party. While the model might be critical, you might not need to see the individual components. All you need for your design is an accurate placeholder for the model.

- **Outgoing Models:** In some cases, you might need to send models to another company, and might not want to send them proprietary Autodesk® Inventor® files. Also, an export file (such as IGES) does not automatically update to reflect future changes. A shrinkwrap part enables you to send your suppliers and vendors associative Autodesk Inventor models, but removes the individual features or components.

*The mass properties of the original file carry over to the shrinkwrap part. To ensure accurate values, it is a good idea to update the mass properties of the original assembly before starting the **Shrinkwrap** command.*

How To: Create a Shrinkwrap Part

1. In the *Assemble* tab>Component panel, click

   (Shrinkwrap). The Create Shrinkwrap Part dialog box opens, as shown in Figure 6–1.

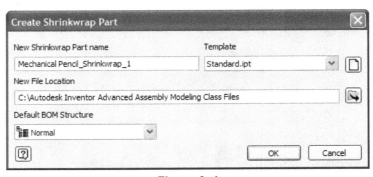

Figure 6–1

2. Change the default options if required and click **OK**.
3. Define the shrinkwrap options using the Assembly Shrinkwrap Options dialog box, as shown in Figure 6–2.

Figure 6–2

- Use the Assembly Shrinkwrap Options dialog box to configure the shrinkwrap part as required. The options are as follows:

Option	Description
Style	This area defines the type of part file that is created.
	• Click ⬚ (Single solid body merging out seams between planar faces) to create a part file that consists of a single solid body that has no edges between planar faces.
	• Click ⬚ (Solid body keep seams between planar faces) to create a part file that consists of a single solid body that has edges between planar faces.
	• Click ⬚ (Maintain each solid as a solid body) to create a multi-body part that contains individual bodies for each part in the assembly.
	• Click ⬚ (Single composite feature) to create a single surface part file. This is the default option and produces the lightest part file.

Preview	Preview the results of the selected shrinkwrap options before generating the part.
Simplification	Use the options in this area to define what geometry is kept in the shrinkwrap part, based on its visibility status in the original component. By default, the **Parts and faces** of the original assembly are kept with a Visibility of 0%. Using this option, all faces that are not exposed in any view orientation are removed from the part. Increase the Visibility percentage to remove parts or faces that have a specified percentage visible in any view orientation removed from the shrinkwrap part.
Remove parts by size	Use this option to remove geometry based on size. When this option is active, any component smaller then the specified percentage of the overall assembly is removed from the shrinkwrap part.
Hole patching	Use this option to remove holes from the shrinkwrap part. By default, all holes are removed from the shrinkwrap part. You can also choose to keep the holes or remove holes of a specified size.
Include other objects	Use the options in this area to specify additional geometric elements to include in the shrinkwrap part. You can also include any visible work geometry, sketches, iMates, and parameters.
Break link	Clear this option to remove the associative link between the shrinkwrap part and the original assembly.
Reduce Memory Mode	When this option is selected, source bodies do not display in the Model Browser of the shrinkwrap part. This option is active by default and helps reduce the memory usage, since the source bodies are not stored in the cache. This option only affects models generated using (Single solid body merging out seams between planar faces) or (Solid body keep seams between planar faces).
Create independent bodies on failed Boolean	Use this option to create a multi-body shrinkwrap part when a single solid body cannot be generated. This option only affects models generated using (Single solid body merging out seams between planar faces) or (Solid body keep seams between planar faces).
Remove all internal voids	Use this option to fill all internal void shells in the shrinkwrap solid body part.

Level of Detail shrinkwrap models have no impact on the Bill of Materials.

4. Click **OK** to generate the Shrinkwrap part. The new shrinkwrap part is automatically created and made active.
5. Save the new part file.

Hint: Shrinkwrapping Components

The **Shrinkwrap** command creates a shrinkwrap part of the active assembly.

- To create a shrinkwrap part of a specific subassembly, activate the subassembly first.

- To create a shrinkwrap part of another part, add the part to an empty assembly, and then shrinkwrap the single part assembly.

- To create a shrinkwrap part that includes only certain components in a subassembly, create and activate a Level of Detail representation that includes only the components required, and then use the **Shrinkwrap** command.

6.2 Assembly Simplification

The assembly Simplification tools can also be used to prepare a model for use in the Autodesk® Revit® software. This functionality is not covered in this chapter.

The assembly Simplification tools provide an alternative to using the **Shrinkwrap** or **Derive Assembly** options to simplify an assembly model to share with others.

To access the simplification tools in the Assembly environment use one of the following:

- Select the *Simplify* tab>Simplify panel (as shown at the top of Figure 6–3).

- Select the *Assemble* tab>Simplify panel (as shown at the bottom of Figure 6–3). This panel is not available by default.

  To display the panel, expand [icon] (Show Panel) at the end of the *Assemble* tab and select **Simplify**.

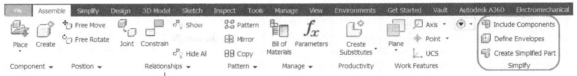

Figure 6–3

Include Components

The **Include Components** simplification tool enables you to create a simplified version of an assembly that includes or excludes selected components.

How To: Include Components in a Simplified View

1. In the *Simplify* tab (or *Assemble* tab)>Simplify panel, click

   [icon] (Include Components). The mini-toolbar opens as shown in Figure 6–4.

These tools enable you to define the selection priority and whether multiple instances of a selected component are also marked for inclusion.

Figure 6–4

2. Select the components for inclusion/exclusion in the simplified model. You can begin selecting components using the default options in the mini-toolbar (**View All/Select Include**). Additional options are described as follows:

- The **View All** option enables you to control whether the model in the graphics window displays all of the components during selection.

- The **View Included** option in the top drop-down list is used to return excluded components back into a Simplified view. The **Select to Exclude** option is automatically enabled once this option is selected and you can select components to exclude them from the Design view.

- The **View Excluded** option in the top drop-down list is used to add excluded components back into a view. They enable you to display only the components that have been selected for inclusion (**View Included**) and select to Exclude, or the components that were selected for exclusion (**View Excluded**).

3. Maintain the defaults in the third row of the mini-toolbar, or customize, as required.

- In the ⬚▼ drop-down list you can define the selection priority to aid in selecting components. Part priority is the default.

- Use ⬚ (Select All Occurrences) option to control whether multiple instances of a selected component are also marked for inclusion.

4. Click ✓ to complete the definition of the simplified part.

Once completed, a view is added to the **View** node in the Model Browser. The default naming scheme for the simplified view is **Simple View#**. The simplified view node can be selected and renamed, as required.

The blower assembly shown on the left in Figure 6–5 displays all of the components while the assembly shown on the right only has a few components selected for inclusion in the Simplified View. The resulting Model Browser is also displayed.

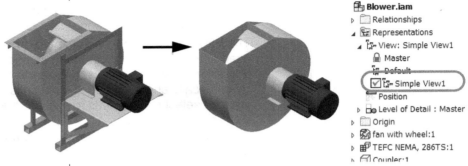

Figure 6–5

To edit a simplified view, right-click on the view name in the Model Browser and select **Edit Include Components**.

- Components can be added or removed using the tools in the mini-toolbar.

- Alternatively, with **View All** selected, you can hold <Ctrl> and select components a second time to clear any previously included components.

To return all of the components to the display, double-click on the **Default** view node in the Model Browser to activate it. The **Simple View#** view is maintained and can be activated as required by double-clicking on it in the Model Browser.

Define Envelopes

The **Define Envelopes** simplification tool enables you to replace a selected component with a bounding box or cylinder.

How To: Create an Envelope to Replace a Component

1. In the *Simplify* tab (or *Assemble* tab)>Simplify panel, click

    (Define Envelopes). The mini-toolbar opens, as shown in Figure 6–6.

*The Define Envelopes command can also be used to simplify components without the use of the **Include Components** tool.*

These tools enable you to define the selection priority, whether multiple instances of a component are marked for inclusion, and if the component is shown or hidden after selection.

This tool enables you to assign a material appearance to the resulting bounding shape.

Figure 6–6

2. Select a component to be replaced by the envelope,
3. Select the bounding shape to replace the selected component. Expand and select **Bounding Box** or **Cylinder** from the drop-down list.
4. Customize the envelope size, if required, to represent a larger area than that of the selected component. Once the bounding box or cylinder has been displayed, select an arrow on a face and drag it to adjust the size, as shown in Figure 6–7. Alternatively, you can enter a value in the field that displays once an arrow has been selected.

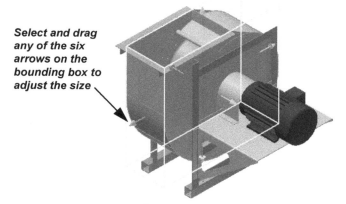

Select and drag any of the six arrows on the bounding box to adjust the size

Figure 6–7

5. Maintain the defaults in the remaining rows of the mini-toolbar or customize, as required.

   - In the drop-down list, you can define the selection priority to aid in selecting components. Part priority is the default.

   - Use (Select All Occurrences) to control whether multiple instances of a selected component are also replaced with the same envelope.

To edit an envelope name after it has been created, right-click on the name in the Model Browser.

- Use the 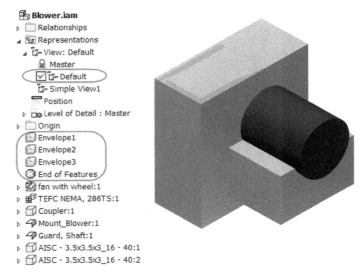 drop-down list to mark the envelope to either show or hide the original selected component once the envelope is created.
- Use the third row of the mini-toolbar to customize the material and appearance of the envelope.

6. Click ✓ to complete the definition of the envelope.

In Figure 6–8, a blower assembly has been simplified using a cylindrical and two box envelopes. The three envelopes are displayed in the Model Browser.

Figure 6–8

Once an envelope is created, it remains displayed unless its visibility is controlled. This is also true in a Simplified view, even if its component is not selected to be included in the Simplified view. To control the display of envelopes, consider the following:

- To temporarily remove envelopes from the model display, drag ⊗ End of Features above them in the list. You can also right-click and select **Suppress Feature**.

- To delete an envelope, right-click and select **Delete Envelope**. It is recommended to delete envelopes that are no longer required in a model, or that were only required to create a simplified version of the model.

> **Hint: Working with Simplified Views and Envelopes**
>
> A Simplified view is not required to create an envelope. However, components that are included in a Simplified view will display the envelope if its component has been selected for inclusion.

Create Simplified Part

The **Create Simplified Part** tool enables you to create a new simplified component. The new part that is created incorporates the active Simplified view, envelopes (displayed or hidden), and any component's visibility that has been disabled. Simplified parts are not associative and do not update if changes are made to the parent assembly's simplified view. If changes are made to the components in the simplified view, any simplified parts created from that view will update

How To: Create a Simplified Part

1. In the *Simplify* tab (or *Assemble* tab)>Simplify panel, click

   (Create Simplified Part). The mini-toolbar opens as shown in Figure 6–9.

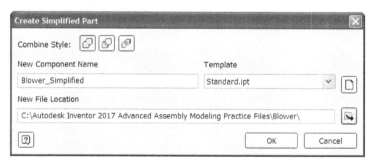

Figure 6–9

2. Select the style for how the generated part should be created.

   - Use to create it as a single solid body with merged seams between the faces.

   - Use to create it as a single solid body with seams maintained.

   - Use to create each solid as a separate solid body.

3. Enter the component's name
4. Select the template to use when creating the new part.

5. Change the default file location, if required.
6. Click **OK** to create the simplified part.

- Once generated, the model opens in a new window. Envelopes that existed in the source assembly are represented as extrusions in the simplified model and can be deleted, if required.

Comparison of Model Simplification Tools

- **Shrinkwrap** enables you to create a single part file that preserves the external surfaces and removes all of the internal data to protect proprietary information. Models in the assembly cannot be individually selected for inclusion/exclusion, but you can remove parts by size, visibility, and patch holes. An associative link between the original assembly and the simplified part file can be maintained.

- **Derive** enables you to create your own part file and populate it with data by deriving geometry from another model. By referencing an existing part or assembly, reusing existing models, sketches, or parameters, etc. you can select the data for your new part. The **Derive** and **Shrinkwrap** options are similar because you can remove parts by size, visibility, and patch holes. However, in the **Derive** option, you can also selectively mark the components in an assembly that are to be derived. You can select a design view, position, or level of detail representation to use when deriving. You can also use boolean operations with the **Derive** option. This process generally maintains an associative link between the final derived part and the original assembly.

- The simplification tools in the *Simplify* tab enable you to customize a simplified assembly by selecting the components to be included. Additionally, you can create envelope geometry to represent components. Using a combination of these tools and model visibility you can create a simplified model using the **Create Simplified Part** option. These tools do not enable you to fill holes in the model. Standard surfacing techniques are required to fill holes once the simplified part has been created. In general, this tool is used for general space claim information. There is no associative link between the original assembly's simplified view and the simplified part file. However, geometry changes to the components in the simplified part will update.

Practice 6a

Creating a Shrinkwrap Model

Practice Objective

• Create an associative shrinkwrap part that can be sent to a vendor.

The Mechanical Pencil assembly needs to be sent to a third party. For proprietary reasons, you do not want to show them the internal workings of the pencil. In this practice, you will create an associative shrinkwrap part that can be sent to the vendor. By creating an associative shrinkwrap model, you can ensure that the shrinkwrap model is always up to date. The mechanical pencil assembly is shown in Figure 6–10.

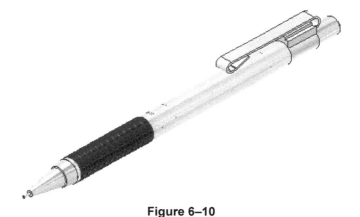

Figure 6–10

Task 1 - Create a shrinkwrap part.

1. Open **Mechanical Pencil.iam** from the *Mechanical_ Pencil_Shrinkwrap* folder.

2. In the *Assemble* tab>expanded Component panel, click

    (Shrinkwrap).

3. Keep the default name and location, click and change the template to **Standard (mm).ipt**, and click **OK**.

4. Click **OK** on the Create Shrinkwrap Part dialog box.

5. In the *Style* area in the Assembly Shrinkwrap Options dialog box, click ⬚ (Solid body keep seams between planar faces).

6. Clear the **Remove parts by size** option.

7. Ensure that the **All** option is selected in the *Hole patching* area in the dialog box and that the **Break link** option is cleared.

8. Click **OK** to generate the shrinkwrap part. The new shrinkwrap model opens automatically.

Task 2 - Review the internal components of the shrinkwrap model.

---

1. Select the *View* tab>Appearance panel and click ⬚ (Half Section View). The command displayed in the drop-down list might vary depending on command that was last selected.

2. Select **YZ Plane** in the Model Browser. Leave the offset value at 0.00. Click ✓. The model is sectioned as shown in Figure 6–11. Note that the interior of the shrinkwrap model is solid.

Figure 6–11

3. Select the *View* tab>Appearance panel and click ⬚ (End Section View).

Task 3 - Make changes to the parent assembly and update the shrinkwrap geometry.

1. Return to the **Mechanical Pencil.iam** window.

2. In the Model Browser, double-click on the **Clip** component to activate it.

3. Show the dimensions for the **Sweep1** feature and edit the *35* dimension value and enter **50**.

4. Activate the top-level assembly.

5. Return to the **Mechanical Pencil_Shrinkwrap_1.ipt** window. Note that the **Mechanical Pencil.iam** derived geometry in the Model Browser has the ⚡ symbol adjacent to it, indicating that it is out-of-date. You might have to move the cursor over the Model Browser to have it update.

6. In the Quick Access Toolbar, click 🔲 to update the shrinkwrap geometry to reflect the change in length to the parent geometry.

*If the **Break Link** option is enabled when the shrinkwrap model is being created, it does not update to reflect the change made to the parent model.*

7. Return to the Mechanical Pencil assembly and edit the *50* dimension value and enter **35**. Update the shrinkwrap model again.

8. Save and close all the open models.

Practice 6b | Creating a Simplified Model

Practice Objectives

- Simplify an assembly model by selecting components for inclusion/exclusion in a Design View.
- Create envelopes of selected parts in an assembly to provide space claim data on the component's size.
- Create a simplified part model that represents a multi component assembly.

In this practice you will create a simplified model to represent the space claims required for a blower assembly. The model will be simplified by selecting components to be included/excluded and envelopes will be created to represent other components. The entire assembly that will be simplified is shown on the left in Figure 6–12 and the simplified model is shown on the right.

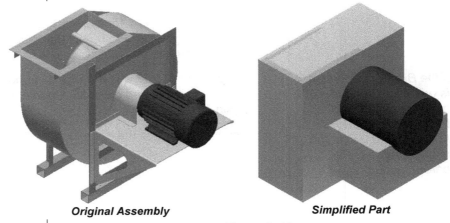

Original Assembly   *Simplified Part*

Figure 6–12

Task 1 - Define the assembly components to be included in the simplified part.

1. Open **Blower.iam** from the *Blower* folder.

2. In the *Simplify* tab>Simplify panel, click (Include Components). The mini-toolbar displays.

3. Select the **Mount_Blower**, **TEFC NEMA**, and **band** components. The band component is located in the fan with wheel>FAN CONSTRAINED subassemblies.

4. Click 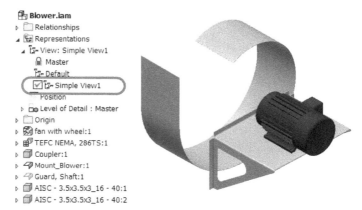 to complete the command. A Design View named **Simple View1** is created in the **View** node, as shown in Figure 6–13. These components form the basis of the envelopes that will be created to represent the assembly in the simplified part.

Figure 6–13

Task 2 - Create envelopes to represent the overall size of the model.

---

1. In the *Simplify* tab>Simplify panel, click (Define Envelopes). The mini-toolbar displays.

2. Expand and click (Bounding Box) if it is not the active selection.

3. Select the **Mount_Blower** part. A default bounding box displays around the model as shown in Figure 6–14, and no adjustments need to be made to the envelope's size.

Figure 6–14

4. Expand 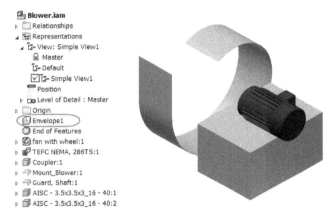 and note that **Hide Original** is active. This ensures that the envelope replaces the selected component. If **Show Original** was selected, both the envelope and the derived geometry for the component would display in the simplified part.

5. Click ✓ to complete the envelope. The model and Model Browser display as shown in Figure 6–15.

Figure 6–15

6. The overall extent of the blower and its frame is not apparent in the current Design View. In the **View** node, right-click on **Simple View1** and select **Edit Include Components**.

7. Select the frame components which define the extents of the assembly, as shown in Figure 6–16. This is done temporarily to create an accurate envelope for the band component.

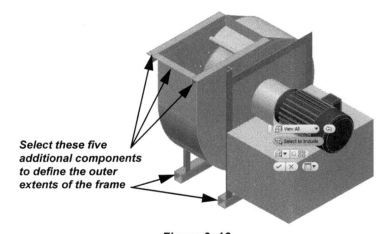

Select these five additional components to define the outer extents of the frame

Figure 6–16

8. Click 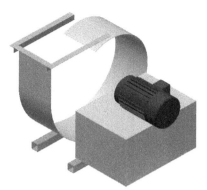 to complete the command. The model displays as shown in Figure 6–17.

Figure 6–17

9. In the *Simplify* tab>Simplify panel, click (Define Envelopes).

10. Select the band component. The **Bounding Box** option is already selected because it was the last shape used.

11. Change to the Front view of the model using the ViewCube. Note that the bounding box does not encompass all of the frame components. The envelope's size can be adjusted as required to represent the true space claim.

12. In the Front view, drag the lower and left arrows to encompass the exterior frame components, as shown in Figure 6–18.

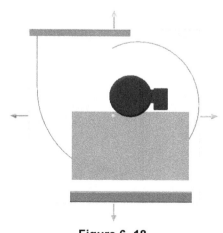

Figure 6–18

13. Navigate to the Top view using the ViewCube. Drag the top and bottom arrows to encompass the frame around the band, as shown in Figure 6–19.

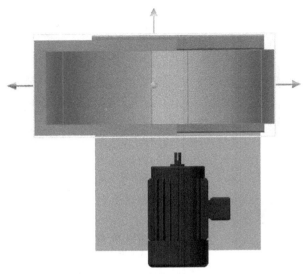

Figure 6–19

14. Maintain the default material for the envelope.

15. Click 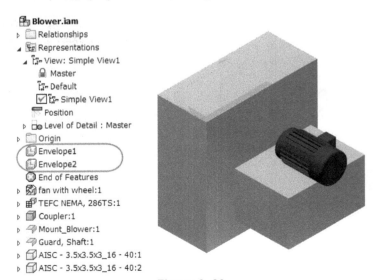 to complete the envelope. The model and Model Browser display as shown in Figure 6–20.

Figure 6–20

16. In the *Simplify* tab>Simplify panel, click 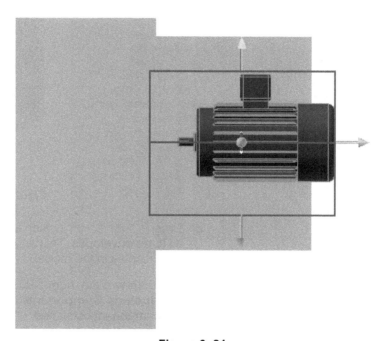 (Define Envelopes).

17. Expand and click (Bounding Cylinder).

18. Select the **TEFC NEMA** component. A bounding cylinder extends around the selected component.

19. Using the ViewCube, change to the Top view of the model. Drag the left arrow so that it extends into the bounding box that represents the housing of the assembly, as shown in Figure 6–21.

Figure 6–21

20. Click 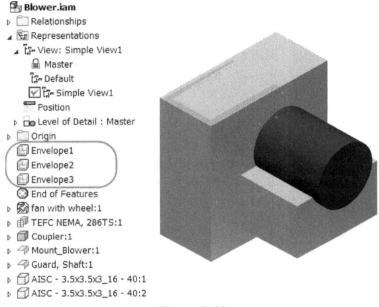 to complete the envelope. The model and Model Browser display as shown in Figure 6–22. Note that three envelopes were created and all of the components still display in the model.

Blower.iam
- ▷ Relationships
- ◢ Representations
  - ◢ View: Simple View1
    - Master
    - Default
    - ☑ Simple View1
    - Position
  - ▷ Level of Detail : Master
  - ▷ Origin
    - Envelope1
    - Envelope2
    - Envelope3
  - End of Features
  - ▷ fan with wheel:1
  - ▷ TEFC NEMA, 286TS:1
  - ▷ Coupler:1
  - ▷ Mount_Blower:1
  - ▷ Guard, Shaft:1
  - ▷ AISC - 3.5x3.5x3_16 - 40:1
  - ▷ AISC - 3.5x3.5x3_16 - 40:2

Figure 6–22

21. Drag ⊗ End of Features (which is below the envelope list), above all three envelopes. This enables you to temporarily toggle off their display in the model.

22. In the **View** node, right-click on **Simple View1** and select **Edit Include Components**. The model displays with all of the components selected.

23. Expand **View All** and click 🔲 (View Included) to only display the components that have been included. Note that the **Mount_Blower**, **TEFC NEMA**, and the band components are no longer included because they have been replaced with envelopes.

*Alternatively, if **View All** is maintained, you can and hold <Ctrl> while selecting components to clear them from inclusion.*

24. **Select to Exclude** becomes active. Select the five frame components to exclude them. If they had remained in the view, they would have been included as derived geometry in the simplified part file that is to be created.

25. Click 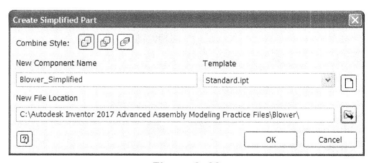 to complete the edit.

26. Drag 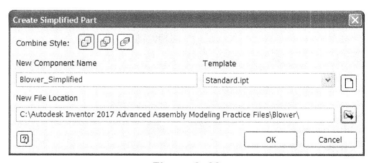 End of Features back to the bottom of the feature list to once again display the envelopes in the model.

Task 3 - Create the simplified part model and modify it.

1. In the *Simplify* tab>Simplify panel, click (Create Simplified Part).

2. In the Create Simplified Part dialog box, change the name for the new component to **Blower_Simplified**.

3. In the *Template* area, browse and select the **Standard(in).ipt** template.

4. In the *New File Location* area, browse and select the *Blower* folder from the practice files folder, if not already specified. The Create Simplified Part dialog box should be as shown in Figure 6–23.

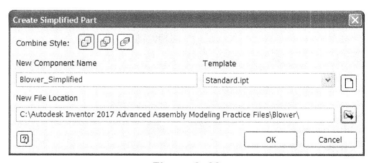

Figure 6–23

5. Click **OK** to create the new part file. The newly created model opens automatically.

6. Review the Model Browser. Note that three extrusions have been added to represent the envelopes that were created to replace the **Mount_Blower**, **TEFC NEMA**, and band components.

7. In the *3D Model* tab>Modify panel, click (Chamfer).

8. Create a chamfer of approximately **20** to represent the true shape of the **Mount_Blower** component, as shown in Figure 6–24.

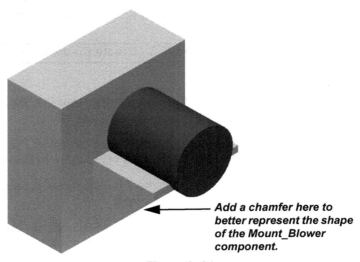

Add a chamfer here to better represent the shape of the Mount_Blower component.

Figure 6–24

9. Save the newly created **Blower_Simplified.ipt** file. It can now be shared with customers for use as a space claim in their designs.

10. Return to the **Blower.iam** window. Save the assembly and close it.

The envelopes that exist in the model can be toggled off by dragging ⊗ End of Features above them. However, if you want to create a new simplified part model with other envelopes, they should be deleted. If they are not deleted, they are included in the simplified part regardless of whether they are toggled off or not.

Chapter Review Questions

1. Which is not a use of a shrinkwrap model in an assembly?

   a. Incoming vendor models

   b. Quickly suppressing all components in an assembly

   c. Outgoing models

   d. Large assembly management

2. Which of the following statements are false for creating a shrinkwrap model. (Select all that apply.)

   a. Any component that is not displayed (visibility toggled off) during shrinkwrap can be automatically removed from the generated shrinkwrap model.

   b. Components are individually selected for inclusion in a shrinkwrap model.

   c. You must manually edit the surface geometry of the model to remove any unwanted holes after the Shrinkwrap model is created.

   d. The Shrinkwrap model is non-associative with the parent geometry; it cannot be associative.

3. Which of the following **View All** options provide the ability to select components for inclusion again once they have been removed? (Select all that apply.)

   a. View All

   b. View Included

   c. View Excluded

4. When an assembly is simplified using (Include Components), which of the following is created in the model and displays in the Model Browser?

   a. Envelope

   b. Simple View

   c. Level of Detail

   d. Positional Representation

5. The second row of options in the Envelope mini-toolbar, shown in Figure 6–25, enables you to do which of the following? (Select all that apply.)

Figure 6–25

a. Set the bounding shape.

b. Set the selection priority.

c. Define the color of the envelope.

d. Determine if all instances of the selected component are also enveloped.

e. Define the selected component as hidden or visible in the simplified part.

6. Only a single component can be selected at one time to be replaced with an envelope using the ![icon] (Define Envelopes) command. The envelope can only represent the exact size of the selected component.

a. True

b. False

7. Which of the following simplification tools can create an associative simplified model that updates if changes are made to the parent assembly? (Select all that apply.)

a. Shrinkwrap

b. Derive

c. Simplified Part

Answers: 1.b, 2.(b,d), 3.(a,c), 4.b, 5.(b,d,e), 6.b, 7.(a,b)

Command Summary

Button	Command	Location
	Create Simplified Part	• **Ribbon:** *Simplify* tab>Simplify panel • **Ribbon:** *Assemble* tab>Simplify panel
	Define Envelopes	• **Ribbon:** *Simplify* tab>Simplify panel • **Ribbon:** *Assemble* tab>Simplify panel
	Include Components	• **Ribbon:** *Simplify* tab>Simplify panel • **Ribbon:** *Assemble* tab>Simplify panel
	Shrinkwrap	• **Ribbon:** *Assemble* tab>Component panel

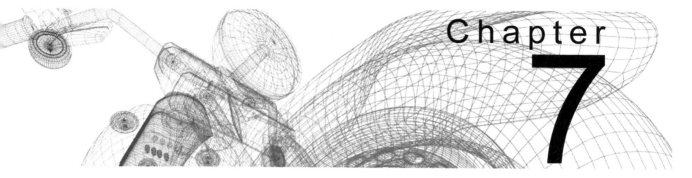

Level of Detail Representations

Level of Detail Representations enable you to save the state of components. They reduce the clutter of large numbers of components, as well as reduce time spent waiting for your system to retrieve a large number of components in an assembly. In general, this tool helps you to work more efficiently with large assemblies.

Learning Objectives in this Chapter

- Display a system-defined Level of Detail (LOD) Representation.
- Simplify the display and create user-defined LOD Representations in an assembly.
- Improve retrieval times for large assemblies by directly opening a LOD Representation where only the required components are loaded or used in a drawing or presentation file.
- Replace a complex component for a simpler one using a Substitute Level of Detail Representation.
- Create a substitute part for every subassembly within the top-level assembly at one time.
- Activate LOD Representations in subassemblies based on naming schemes.

7.1 Level of Detail Representations

Level of Detail (LOD) Representations are used to improve assembly retrieval times, simplify the display of the assembly, and improve the capacity and performance when working with larger assemblies. Three examples are shown in Figure 7–1.

Master LOD Representation   **User-Defined LOD Representation**   **User-Defined LOD Representation**

Figure 7–1

- You can create LOD Representations that only display and load the components you need to work with at any given time. This is done by suppressing components you do not need, and creating and saving an LOD that can be activated at any time.

- Retrieval times for larger assemblies are improved by using an LOD that does not load all the components before opening the assembly. After retrieval of an LOD in an assembly, you can unsuppress (load) and suppress (unload) any additional components as required and then create a new LOD to store the new assembly state.

- LODs can be used in drawings and presentations. Design View and Positional Representations can also be used in conjunction with LODs.

Capacity Meter

LOD Representations are often used to manage the amount of memory used by the software by only loading required assembly components for a design task. The Capacity Meter located in the lower-right corner of the screen is used to monitor the amount of memory used by the software. The Capacity Meter is shown in Figure 7–2.

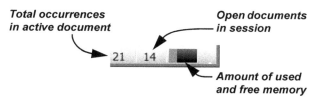

Figure 7–2

- The amount of used and free memory area in the Capacity Meter is not available in 64-bit operating systems.

7.2 System-Defined Level of Detail Representations

Assemblies have four system-defined LOD Representations that are automatically created. System-defined LOD Representations cannot be modified, but you can copy them and modify the copy to create new ones. To access the system-defined LODs, in the Model Browser, expand the *Representations* folder and the Level of Detail branch, as shown in Figure 7–3.

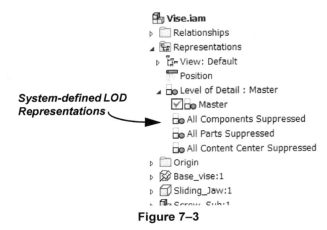

Figure 7–3

Double-click on any of the system-defined representations underneath Level of Detail to activate it.

*Alternatively, you can right-click on the LOD Representation and select **Activate**.*

- **The Master** LOD Representation contains the default state of the assembly, where all components are loaded (unsuppressed).

- The **All Components Suppressed** LOD Representation suppresses all parts and subassemblies in the assembly.

- The **All Parts Suppressed** LOD Representation suppresses all parts in the assembly, including those in subassemblies. The subassembly structure is still visible in the Model Browser.

- The **All Content Center Suppressed** LOD Representation suppresses all Content Center items.

7.3 User-Defined Level of Detail Representations

You can create user-defined LOD Representations in an assembly. This is done by activating the Master or LOD Representation that most closely matches the one you want to create. For example, if you want to create one that suppresses the majority of the components in the assembly, activate the All Components Suppressed LOD so that you only need to unsuppress the few components you need to work with.

How To: Create an LOD Representation

Alternatively, you can right-click on the LOD Representation you want to copy and select **Copy**.

1. With the required LOD Representation activated, in the Model Browser, right-click on the Level of Detail branch and select **New Level of Detail**.
   - A new LOD is created, as shown in Figure 7–4.
   - Any components suppressed in the previously activated LOD are also suppressed in the new LOD Representation.

To help locate components for suppression or unsuppression, use the Selection Priority tool in the Quick Access Toolbar.

Figure 7–4

2. With the new LOD Representation active, suppress and unsuppress components to define the LOD as required.
3. Rename the LOD Representation using a descriptive name by clicking it twice (not double-clicking) in the Model Browser and entering the new name.
4. Save the assembly to save the new LOD Representation.

You can make changes to the LOD Representation once it is created. Activate it, suppress and unsuppress the required components, and resave the assembly.

7.4 Using Level of Detail Representations

LOD Representations can be used during assembly retrieval, when creating drawing views, and in presentation files.

Assembly Retrieval

LOD Representations improve retrieval times for large assemblies. By directly opening an LOD Representation other than the default Master LOD Representation, only the required components are loaded into the software.

How To: Open an LOD Representation During Assembly Retrieval

1. In the Quick Access Toolbar, click ⬚ or use one of the other options to open the Open dialog box.
2. Select the assembly and click **Options**. The File Open Options dialog box opens.
3. Select the required LOD Representation from the *Level of Detail Representation* drop-down list.
4. Click **OK** in the File Open Options dialog box and click **Open** in the Open dialog box. The Assembly opens with the selected LOD Representation activated.

Hint: Setting a default LOD Representation

You can specify a default LOD Representation to retrieve when the assembly is next opened:

1. In the Application Options dialog box, select the *File* tab and click **File Open Options**.
2. Select the required LOD in the Level of Detail Representation drop-down list.

By default, Autodesk Inventor is set to open the last active LOD. Changing this setting reduces the chance that you might open the master representation in error, taking valuable time to open many unnecessary components.

Drawings

Any LOD Representation can be selected for use while creating or modifying a base drawing view, or while modifying a projected Isometric drawing view. When creating a base view, select the required LOD Representation, as shown in Figure 7–5. To change the LOD Representation used in a base view or projected isometric view, right-click, select **Edit View**, and select the LOD.

Select the required LOD Representation here.

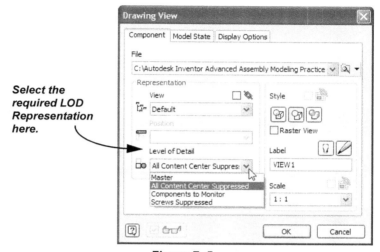

Figure 7–5

Presentations

Any LOD Representation can be selected for use while creating a view in a Presentation file by clicking **Options** and selecting the LOD Representation.

7.5 Substitute Level of Detail Representations

A Substitute Level of Detail (LOD) enables you to swap out a complex component for a simpler one that represents it. The substitute still contains all of the BOM information that is normally associated with the assembly, as well as the physical information (such as center of gravity and mass). Using substitute parts reduces the amount of components loaded into memory, as well as the number of constraints and adaptive relationships that must be recalculated when changes are made. By simplifying the model, the intention of a Substitute Level of Detail is to reduce the computing resources and thereby increase performance without sacrificing access to BOM information.

The model on the left in Figure 7–6 shows the Master Representation for an assembly. A Substitute Level of Detail for the fan and its electronic components is shown on the right.

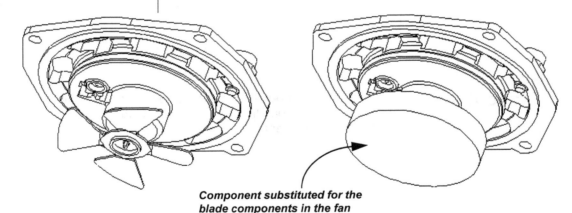

Component substituted for the blade components in the fan

Figure 7–6

How To: Create a Substitute LOD

1. Open the subassembly that is to be simplified. This assembly is called the Owning Assembly.
2. (Optional) Create a reduced-part LOD Representation. In this LOD, suppress any of those components in the subassembly that are to be removed to simplify the assembly.
3. In the Model Browser, right-click on the LOD and select **New Substitute.** Select one of the three options shown in Figure 7–7: **Derive Assembly**, **Shrinkwrap**, or **Select Part File**.

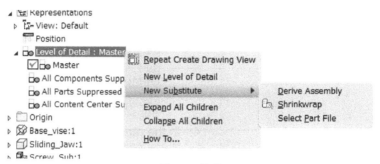

Figure 7–7

- The **Derive Assembly** option simplifies the assembly using the Derived Component functionality. A new part file is created that is then substituted for the assembly in the Level of Detail. The derived part is created in the same way as one that uses the Derive tool. You define its name, template, and location, and then use the Derived Assembly dialog box to control which components are included in the new part file. The new Substitute LOD is created using the new derived part file.

- The **Shrinkwrap** command creates a shrinkwrap part of the active assembly and creates a Level of Detail that uses it. The shrinkwrap part is created in the same way as one that uses the Shrinkwrap tool. After you define its name, template, and location, you use the Assembly Shrinkwrap Options dialog box to control how the shrinkwrap is created. The new shrinkwrap part is automatically created, and a Substitute LOD of the shrinkwrap for the top-level assembly is created.

Hint: Working with Shrinkwraps

- Individual parts cannot be shrinkwrapped.

- To create a shrinkwrap part of a specific subassembly inside the top-level assembly, you must first open it explicitly (cannot be edited and created in place) and perform a Shrinkwrap LOD from the *Representations* folder in that assembly. After saving and returning to the master subassembly, the lower level shrinkwrap LOD is available for selection in a higher level LOD.

- The **Select Part File** option substitutes a single part file for the assembly. Selecting **Select Part File** substitutes a selected file for the assembly in the Level of Detail. The part file can be a previously simplified assembly, shrinkwrap model, or another part file. After you select this option you are prompted to select a component. The Substitute LOD is created using the selected part file.

4. In the main assembly, create a new LOD and activate Substitute LOD in any subassemblies, as required.

7.6 LOD Productivity Tools

Three of the productivity tools—**Create Substitutes**, **Update Substitutes**, and **Link Levels of Detail**—can be used to help you more efficiently work with large assemblies and levels of details. The commands are shown in Figure 7–8.

*All productivity tools are grouped in the Productivity panel. To display all commands in the main panel, right-click on the command that is displayed in the main panel and select **Ungroup Commands from Drop-Down Menu**.*

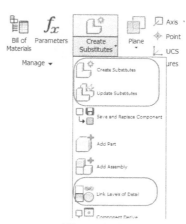

Figure 7–8

Create Substitutes

The **Create Substitutes** option creates a substitute part for every subassembly within the top-level assembly.

How To: Create Substitutes

1. In the *Assemble* tab>Productivity panel, click (Create Substitutes). The Create Substitutes dialog box opens as shown in Figure 7–9.

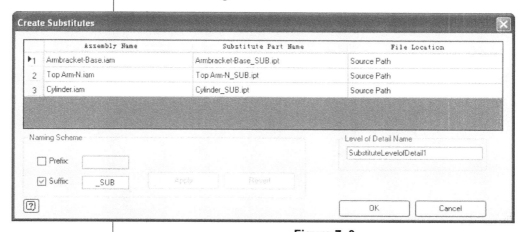

Figure 7–9

*If there is a subassembly that you do not want to substitute, right-click on its row in the Create Substitutes dialog box and select **Remove Row**.*

2. Modify the *Substitute Part Name* column, as required, to name the part file that is going to be generated for each subassembly.

   - By default, all substitute parts have the suffix **_SUB**.
   - You can change the name of the substitute parts by clicking inside the appropriate row and entering a new value.
   - You can also change the suffix or add a prefix to all substitute parts using the *Naming Scheme* area of the dialog box.

3. Enter the LOD Representation name in the *Level of Detail Name* field that will be used in each as subassembly and at the top level.

4. Click **OK**. When prompted that you have chosen to create substitutes, click **Yes**.

The substitute parts and the LOD Representations are generated. In addition, the LOD Representations that replace the subassemblies with their substitute parts are activated, as shown in Figure 7–10.

Use the new productivity tool

(Link Levels of Detail) to quickly switch between the Level of Detail representations.

Figure 7–10

Update Substitutes

The **Update Substitutes** option ( ) updates all of the substitute parts in an assembly in a single operation. This command quickly updates all substitute parts created when using the **Create Substitutes** command, and ensures that the substitute part still accurately reflects the subassembly from which it was derived.

Link Levels of Detail

The **Link Levels of Detail** option ( ) activates any Level of Detail (LOD) representations within subassemblies that have the same name as the selected Level of Detail in the top-level assembly. This tool makes activating level of details at multiple levels in an assembly much faster, since you do not need to manually activate LODs at multiple levels.

> **Hint: LODs in Templates**
>
> You should consider adding LODs to the assembly templates. This automatically creates all system-defined LODs and can include any company-specific LODs that are consistently used in your company's designs (e.g., low, medium, or high). Using LODs in the template can help reduce the time spent creating the LODs in assemblies and subassemblies, and ensure consistent naming conventions for use with the **Link Levels of Detail** command.

Practice 7a

Level of Detail Representations

Practice Objective

- Simplify the display and minimize the number of components loaded in a session by creating and using LOD representations for an assembly.

LOD Representations are generally used for larger assemblies.

In this practice, you create and use LOD Representations for the vise assembly shown in Figure 7–11. The design intent is to simplify the display and minimize the number of components loaded in a session.

Figure 7–11

Task 1 - Open an assembly file.

1. Open **Vise.iam** from the *LevelOfDetailRepresentations* folder.

2. In the Model Browser, expand the *Representations* folder and expand the Level of Detail branch, as shown in Figure 7–12. The four system-defined LOD Representations are listed and are available for use. All assemblies contain these by default.

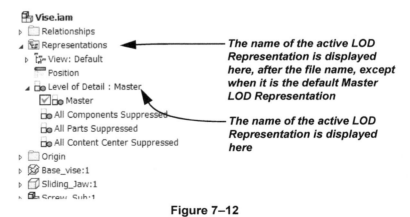

Figure 7–12

The numbers in the Capacity Meter might vary depending on the number of additional files you have open.

3. Look at the Capacity Meter at the bottom-right corner of the Autodesk Inventor window, as shown in Figure 7–13. It displays the number of occurrences in the document and the number of documents in session. Hold the cursor over the amount of used and free memory and note the amounts for each. The amount of used and free memory area in the Capacity Meter is not available in 64-bit operating systems.

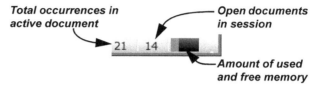

Total occurrences in active document

Open documents in session

Amount of used and free memory

Figure 7–13

4. Activate the **All Components Suppressed** LOD Representation. All components are suppressed. Review the Capacity Meter again. The number of occurrences is now zero, the number of open documents is one, and the amount of used memory has decreased slightly. The amount of memory used decreases more significantly for larger assemblies when using LOD Representations with suppressed components.

Task 2 - Create an LOD Representation.

Several screws in the assembly are not significant to its design. To be able to easily switch between an assembly state that contains the screws and one that does not load the screws, you can create an LOD Representation that suppresses all the screws. The difference in memory used might not be significant for a smaller assembly such as this, but it can make a difference for assemblies that contain a large number of screws, nuts, washers, etc.

Before you create an LOD Representation, decide if it is better to begin creating the LOD Representation with all the components suppressed, all components unsuppressed, or somewhere in between. If you are working with a large assembly and the components you want to keep unsuppressed are only a small portion compared to the rest of the assembly, then you can begin by suppressing all components first. In this situation, the assembly is small and the number of components you must suppress is smaller than the total number of components in the assembly, so you will create an LOD Representation based on the Master LOD Representation.

To save the visibility status of components in an assembly, use Design View Representations.

1. Right-click on the Master LOD Representation and select **Copy**. A new LOD Representation is added to the list, called **Master1**.

2. In the Model Browser, click twice (do not double-click) on **Master1** and rename it as **Screws Suppressed**.

3. Double-click on **Screws Suppressed**, if it is not already activated.

4. Select the six screws in the assembly, right-click, and select **Suppress**. There is no visible change in the graphics window, because the screws are hidden behind components in the assembly. The Model Browser displays as shown in Figure 7–14.

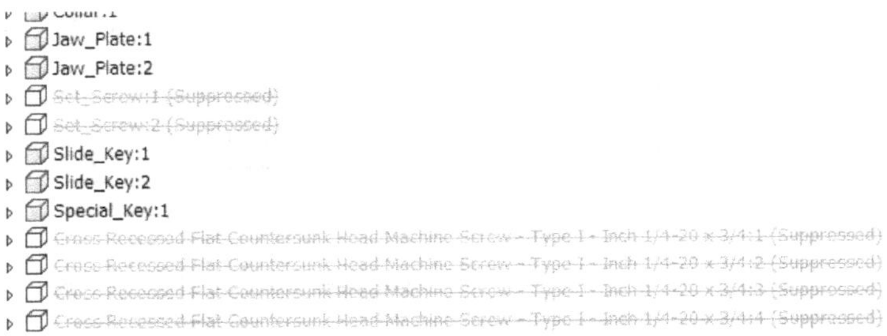

Figure 7–14

5. Save the assembly to save the LOD Representation and the changes that you made to it.

Task 3 - Create a second LOD Representation to help you make modifications in a particular area.

When you continually return to a particular area in the assembly to make modifications or inspect more closely, you can create an LOD Representation that loads only those components that are required for reference and modification. In such situations, without the use of LOD Representations, a simple modification or inspection of a small area in a large assembly could result in unnecessarily long retrieval times and a significant reduction in productivity. In the vise assembly, you want to take a closer look at the Collar.

1. Activate the **All Components Suppressed** LOD Representation. Because the majority of the components will be suppressed in this LOD Representation, you should begin with the All Components Suppressed LOD Representation.

2. With All Components Suppressed activated, in the Model Browser, right-click on the Level of Detail branch, as shown in Figure 7–15, and select **New Level of Detail**. A new LOD Representation is created and all components should be suppressed.

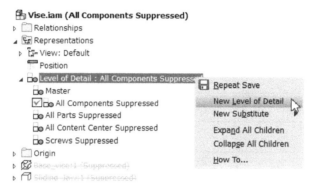

Figure 7–15

3. Rename the new LOD Representation as **Components to Monitor**.

4. Select **Collar:1** and **Special_Key:1**, right-click, and select **Suppress**. This will unsuppress **Collar:1** and **Special_Key:1**.

You want to unsuppress one additional component and it is in the **Screw_Sub:1** subassembly. Note that the components in the subassembly cannot be viewed because the subassembly is suppressed.

5. Select the **Screw_Sub:1** subassembly, right-click, and select **Suppress** to unsuppress the subassembly.

6. Expand the **Screw_Sub:1** subassembly. **Vise_Screw:1** is the only component required to be visible. Suppress all components in the subassembly, except for **Vise_Screw:1**. The Model Browser and model display as shown in Figure 7–16.

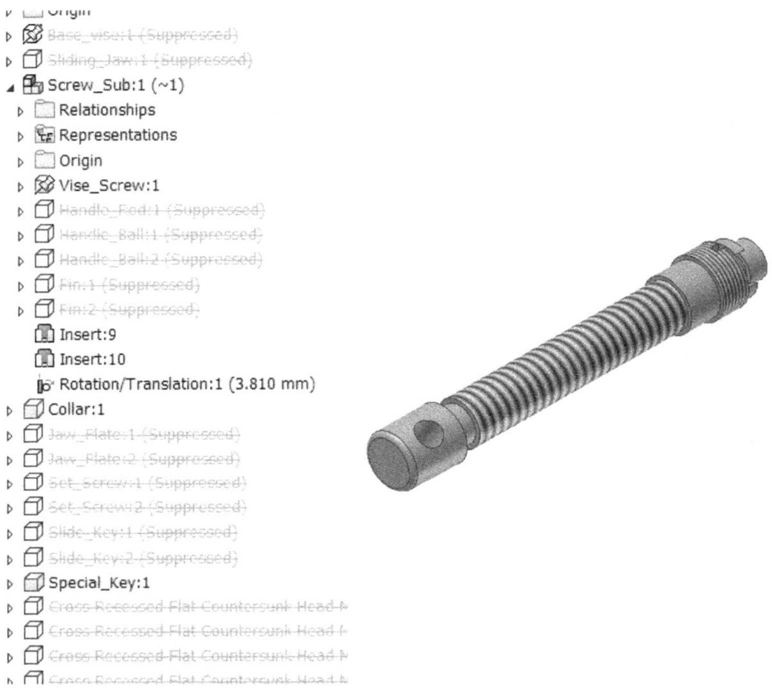

Figure 7–16

7. Rotate and zoom into the model, as shown in Figure 7–17.

Figure 7–17

8. Save the assembly to save the LOD information. The LOD Representation just created focuses on this area and loads only these components.

9. Close the assembly.

Task 4 - Open the Vise assembly LOD Representation.

To help reduce retrieval time, select an LOD Representation other than the default Master.

1. In the Quick Access Toolbar, click [image]. The Open dialog box opens.

2. In the *LevelOfDetailRepresentations* folder, select **Vise.iam** and click **Options**. The File Open Options dialog box opens.

3. In the File Open Options dialog box, in the *Level of Detail Representation* drop-down list, select **Components to Monitor**.

4. In the File Open Options dialog box, click **OK** and then in the Open dialog box, click **Open**. The Assembly opens with the Components to Monitor LOD Representation activated. By using this method of opening the assembly, you have reduced the number of components loaded in session and can immediately access the components that you need.

5. Close the model.

Practice 7b

Substitute Level of Detail

Practice Objective

- Reduce the number of components loaded into memory by creating and activating multiple Substitute Level of Details using the Derive Assembly and Select Part File options.

In this practice, you create and activate multiple Substitute Level of Details, as shown in Figure 7–18. The first Substitute Level of Detail uses the **Derive Assembly** option. The second Substitute Level of Detail uses the **Select Part File** option. The design intent is to reduce the number of components loaded into memory.

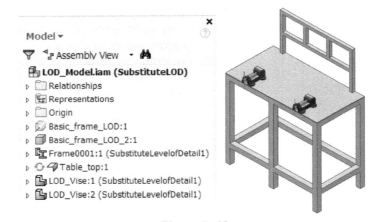

Figure 7–18

Task 1 - Create a Substitute Level of Detail using Derive Assembly.

1. Open **LOD_Model.iam** from the *Substitute LOD* folder.

2. Note the number of components in the capacity meter. There are 71 total occurrences in this assembly and 42 individual documents open, as shown in Figure 7–19. The amount of memory used by the software varies depending on what operations have been executed in the software.

Figure 7–19

The amount of used and free memory area in the Capacity Meter is not available in 64-bit operating systems.

3. In the Model Browser, right-click on **Frame0001:1** and select **Open**. Note the number of components loaded in the Capacity Meter, as shown in Figure 7–20.

Figure 7–20

4. Expand the *Representations* folder and expand the Level of Detail branch.

5. Right-click on **Level of Detail: Master** and select **New Substitute>Derive Assembly**. The New Derived Substitute Part dialog box opens.

6. Keep the default values and click **OK**. The substitute component is created in the same directory as your working assembly is. The Derived Assembly dialog box opens.

7. In the Derived Assembly dialog box, select all of the components in **Frame0001.iam** (do not select the top-level assembly). Click the ⬚ button at the top of the dialog box or the icon next to the components to set them to Bounding Box, as shown in Figure 7–21 and click **OK**. This changes the status for all components in the assembly, but does not change the status of the assembly. A Substitute Level of Detail is created for the frame assembly containing simplified versions of all components.

Figure 7–21

8. Note the number of components loaded in the Capacity Meter, as shown in Figure 7–22. The frame assembly has been reduced to a single component.

Figure 7–22

9. Save and close **Frame0001.iam**.

Task 2 - Use the Substitute Level of Detail in the main assembly.

1. Return to the **LOD_Model.iam** window.

2. In the Model Browser, expand **Frame0001.iam**, then the *Representations* folder, then the Level of Detail branch.

3. Right-click on **SubstituteLevelofDetail1** and select **Activate**. The Substitute Level of Detail for the frame subassembly is loaded. The number of individual components is reduced from 71 to 49, and the number of unique occurrences is reduced from 42 to 20, as shown in Figure 7–23.

Figure 7–23

4. Save **LOD_Model.iam**. The Save Level of Detail Representation Changes dialog box opens. Type **SubstituteLOD** for the name and click **Yes**. A new Level of Detail Representation is created in the top-level assembly that uses the Substitute for the frame subassembly.

5. Expand the *Representations* folder and the Level of Detail branch for **LOD_Model.iam**. The Level of Detail Representation you created is set as active.

Task 3 - Create a Substitute Level of Detail using Select Part File.

1. In the Model Browser, right-click on **LOD_Vise:1** and select Open. The **LOD_Vise** assembly contains 21 total occurrences, as shown in Figure 7–24.

Figure 7–24

2. Expand the *Representations* folder and the Level of Detail branch.

3. Right-click on **Level of Detail: Master** and select **New Substitute>Select Part File**. The Place Component dialog box opens.

4. Select **Vise_Substitute.ipt** in the *Substitute_LOD* folder and click **Open**.

5. Click **Yes** in the Warning dialog box. **Vise_Substitute.ipt** is flagged as a substitute component.

6. Note the number of components loaded in the Capacity Meter, as shown in Figure 7–25. The vise assembly has been reduced to a single component.

Figure 7–25

7. Save and close **LOD_Vise.iam**.

Task 4 - Use the Substitute Level of Detail in the main assembly.

---

1. In the Model Browser, ensure that the **SubstituteLOD** Level of Detail is active for **LOD_Model.iam**.

2. In the Model Browser, expand **LOD_Vise:1**, then the *Representations* folder, then the Level of Detail branch.

3. Right-click on **SubstituteLevelofDetail1** and select **Activate**. The Substitute Level of Detail for the vise subassembly is loaded. The number of individual components is reduced from 49 to 29, as shown in Figure 7–26.

Figure 7–26

4. Expand **LOD_Vise:2**, then the *Representations* folder, then the Level of Detail branch.

5. Activate **SubstituteLevelofDetail1** for **LOD_Vise:2**. The number of individual components is reduced from 29 to 9, as shown in Figure 7–27. The assembly has been simplified from 71 occurrences to 9 with only 8 unique files open.

Figure 7–27

6. Save and close **LOD_Model.iam**.

Practice 7c

Shrinkwrap & Level of Detail

Practice Objectives

- Increase system performance by removing detail from an assembly by creating and using a Level of Detail representation that substitutes a shrinkwrap part.
- Control Level of Detail representations that exist in subassemblies from the top-level assemblies in which they reside.

In this practice, you will use Shrinkwrap and Level of Detail functionality to work on the mechanical pencil assembly shown in Figure 7–28.

Figure 7–28

Task 1 - Create a Level of Detail Representation using a shrinkwrap part.

In this task, you will remove some detail from the grip component by creating a new Level of Detail representation that substitutes the Housing subassembly for a shrinkwrap part. This functionality is useful when working with large assemblies. By removing some of the detail in an assembly, you can increase system performance.

1. Open **Mechanical Pencil.iam** from the *Mechanical_ Pencil_Shrinkwrap* folder.

2. Right-click on the Housing subassembly and select **Open**.

3. Double-click on the **Grip** component to activate it.

4. Suppress **Extrusion1** and **Circular Pattern1**.

5. Activate and save the Housing assembly.

6. In the Model Browser, expand the *Representations* folder. Right-click on **Level of Detail : Master** and select **New Substitute>Shrinkwrap**.

7. Keep the default name and location. Use the **Standard (mm).ipt** template.

8. Click **OK**. The Assembly Shrinkwrap Options dialog box opens.

9. In the *Style* area in the dialog box, click 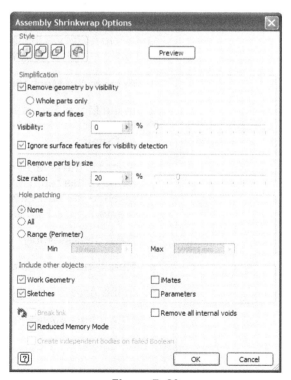 (Single composite feature) and click **Preview**.

10. By default, all holes are patched. In this case, this is not desirable. In the *Hole patching* area in the dialog box, select the **None** option and click **Preview**.

11. Remove the ring component from the shrinkwrap part by enabling the **Remove parts by size** option and setting the *Size ratio* to **20%**, as shown in Figure 7–29. Any part in the assembly that is less then 20% of the overall assembly size will now be excluded from the shrinkwrap part.

Figure 7–29

12. Click **Preview** again to view the changes.

13. Click **OK** to generate the shrinkwrap part. The shrinkwrap part and a new Level of Detail representation is created. Note that the suppressed features were not generated in the shrinkwrap part.

14. Save the model.

15. Activate the Master Level of Detail representation and unsuppress **Extrusion1** and **Circular Pattern1** from **Grip.ipt**.

16. Save the model.

17. Switch between the Master and the **SubstituteLevelofDetail1** Level of Detail representations to view the difference.

18. Ensure that the Master Level of Detail representation is active.

Task 2 - Link Level of Detail Representations.

In this task, you will use the productivity tool, **Link Levels of Detail**, to quickly substitute the shrinkwrap part (created in the last task) into the top-level assembly.

1. Activate the Mechanical Pencil window.

2. In the Model Browser, expand the *Representations* folder. Right-click on **Level of Detail : Master** and select **New Level of Detail**.

3. Rename the level of detail as **SubstituteLevelofDetail1**. The name of this representation needs to match exactly what was given to the new Level of Detail representation that was created in the Housing subassembly.

4. Save the assembly.

5. Reactivate the Master Level of Detail representation.

6. In the *Assemble* tab>expanded Productivity panel, click (Link Levels of Detail).

7. In the Link Levels of Detail dialog box, select
   SubstituteLevelofDetail1, as shown in Figure 7–30, and
   click **OK**.

Figure 7–30

8. Click **OK** to the warning. The **SubstituteLevelofDetail1** in
   both the top-level assembly and the housing subassembly
   activate.

9. Use the **Link Levels of Detail** command again to reactivate
   the Master Level of Detail in both the top-level assembly and
   the subassemblies.

   In this example, you could have manually activated the
   SubstituteLevelofDetail1 Level of Detail representation in
   the Housing subassembly, and then viewed the substitution
   without creating the top-level representation and using the
   Link Level of Details command. When you have more than
   one representation of the same name in multiple
   subassemblies and in the top-level assembly, this tool can be
   a great time-saver.

10. Save all of the open models.

Chapter Review Questions

1. What is a benefit of adding Level of Detail Representations to an assembly. (Select all that apply.)

   a. Displays and loads only the components you need to work on.

   b. Changes component positions.

   c. Simplifies the display of an assembly by removing unnecessary components.

   d. Improves retrieval times of larger assemblies.

2. You can manipulate the four system-defined LOD representations.

   a. True

   b. False

3. How do you open an assembly so that only the components in a selected user-defined LOD Representation are displayed?

   a. Save the assembly with the specific LOD Representation active.

   b. Application Menu, Open LOD Representation.

   c. In the File Open Options dialog box, **Level of Detail Representation** menu.

4. Representations can be used in Drawings but not Presentations.

   a. True

   b. False

5. How can you verify the effect a Substitute LOD has on memory usage?

   a. Model Browser

   b. Windows Explorer

   c. Ribbon

   d. Capacity Meter

Answers: 1.(a,c,d), 2.b, 3.c, 4.b, 5.d

Command Summary

Button	Command	Location
	Create Substitutes	• **Ribbon:** *Assemble* tab>Productivity panel
	Link Levels of Detail	• **Ribbon:** *Assemble* tab>Productivity panel
	Update Substitutes	• **Ribbon:** *Assemble* tab>Productivity panel

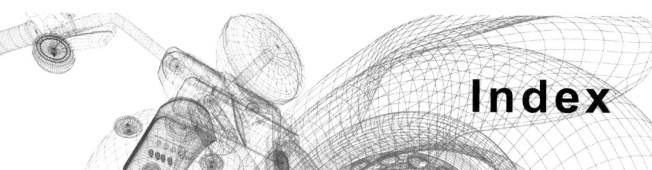

Index

www.ingramcontent.com/pod-product-compliance
Lightning Source LLC
Chambersburg PA
CBHW060536060326
40690CB00017B/3504